THE TEACHER LIBERATION HANDBOOK

THE TEACHER LIBERATION HANDBOOK

How to Leave School and Create a Place Where You and Young People Can Thrive

Joel Hammon

ISBN-13: 9780997978001
ISBN 10: 0997978007
Library of Congress Control Number: 2016915089
Grelton Group, Langhorne, PA

Praise for The Teacher Liberation Handbook

For all those teachers out there who know in their hearts that far too many of our children are disengaged and disenfranchised in school, Joel Hammon has written a powerful roadmap for change that puts kids at the center of their learning and redefines what a "school" might be. – Will Richardson, author of *Why School?*, *Freedom to Learn* and *Personal Learning Networks*

In the words of Derek Sivers, Joel Hammon is the "First Follower" of this approach, turning me from a "Lone Nut" into some sort of "Leader." Joel's vision, determination, and genuine concern for young people has inspired me to continue my own work and pushed me to be more serious and thoughtful along the way. His optimism and character shine throughout his storytelling. This book is a gift from Joel to the many disillusioned teachers who dream of starting their own programs. The world needs your action! – Kenneth Danford, co-founder and director of North Star: Self-Directed Learning for Teens

The Teacher Liberation Handbook shows you how to transform your life as an educator, find real autonomy, promote self-directed learning, and build respectful relationships with the young people you serve. Don't wait for the school system to change; go change it yourself by creating a powerful alternative like Joel. - Blake Boles, author of *The Art of Self-Directed Learning* and *Better Than College*

Contents

have a lot of family and friends who are teachers or retired teachers. In the past ten years, I don't remember a conversation I've had with them, or any other teacher, in which they spoke positively about their jobs, said they were inspired by what was happening in their schools, or said that they were happy most days going to work.

Are you a teacher? Do you love working with kids but are frustrated by the system in which you work? Do you wish there was a way to work with young people in a meaningful and purposeful way that would allow you to bring your own creativity and passions to the job without having to deal with all the regulations handed down from the department, district, state, and federal government?

Perhaps I just hang around the wrong teachers, or perhaps there is a pervasive feeling within the profession that something is not quite right. We went into teaching to inspire and open up possibilities for young people but find ourselves dealing mostly with tests and standardized curriculum, directives from the higher-ups, and teacher evaluation systems that make no sense. We know how to support kids, but that is not what we are asked to do on a daily basis. Our expertise and knowledge is disregarded, ignored, and pushed to the side as the national conversation about education turns more and more to standardization and testing.

I was there. I taught for more than ten years, and by the end, I couldn't shake the feeling that what I did each day was mostly making young people who didn't want to be there in the first place do things they didn't want to do. I felt like I was part of a system that, far from helping kids learn and grow, was actually preventing learning and growth in many cases. This is not a pleasant way to go through life and certainly not why I went into teaching.

Many teachers feel trapped. If you like working with kids but don't like working in schools, what can you do? What jobs and paths are open to you?

When I reached my lowest in the profession, when I knew I had to get out, I started asking these kinds of questions. At first I found no good answers. Then I found North Star: Self-Directed Learning for Teens. It was a godsend. This program in Massachusetts has pioneered a model that allows educators to leave their jobs and create centers that promote self-directed learning for young people. It allows the adults working there to bring all their talents, energy, and creativity to the work of helping young people make lives and educations for themselves, and still make a living. The best part of all is that you are the final decision maker about how you spend your time, and you control the way you interact with young people.

With North Star's example as a guide, I helped cofound the Princeton Learning Cooperative in 2010, where I am currently on staff. I love my work here. I'm excited almost every day to do what I do. I could not say that when I was a teacher.

My life is immeasurably better.

North Star gets a lot of calls and e-mails from frustrated teachers who are inspired by what the program is doing and want to know how to start a program in their own communities. They got so many inquiries that staff and board members from North Star and staff from the Princeton Learning Cooperative decided to start a nonprofit organization, Liberated Learners, to coordinate and support the creation of North Star model centers all over the world. As of this writing, we have ten centers operating in our network and three in the start-up phase.

This is why I decided to write this book. Just as there are many young people who feel trapped in school, there are many teachers who also feel trapped in school. I think we have found a way out for both teachers and their students. I want to share what I have learned so that other teachers can create their own programs and improve the quality of their own work and lives.

I'm happy to continue the conversation at me@joelhammon.com. You can find more information at www.joelhammon.com.

1

Contrasts

What stands out the most when comparing my teaching career to the work I do now at the Princeton Learning Cooperative are the contrasts: the way I relate to the young people I work with, how I feel about what I am doing, how I spend my time, the meaning of what I do. To give you a sense of what these contrasts are, I offer a couple memories from my time teaching and my time at PLC.

PUBLIC MIDDLE SCHOOL OUTSIDE PHILADELPHIA
November 2007, 10:41 a.m.

I walk to the guidance office to participate in a "team meeting" conference. We had summoned the family of one of our seventh-grade students who was not performing well in any of his core academic classes in an effort to fix the situation. Four teachers (including me), a guidance counselor, the principal, and a social worker are assembled in a tiny conference room as we await the family's arrival. As the student's parents enter and take their seats, the guidance counselor talks about why we have called this meeting: We want the best for you ... We know you can be doing better ... just want to figure out what is going on so we can help you be successful...

As thirteen-year-old Dylan looks up, he sees almost all of the adult authority figures in his life staring back at him. This is serious. We start with a status report from each of the teachers, who hold printouts of the grade sheets for their classes—lists of assignments, the points earned on each, and his current grade in the class.

The science teacher goes first: You're missing eight assignments that you have received zero points for. You still need to make up this test, which when that is done will likely help. These quizzes are easy and designed to help boost your grade, but you've been getting 50 percent on them, so they are actually hurting you. Just a little bit of study should do it. Overall, right now you are at a 44 percent.

Now English: You're missing this many. You did poorly on these tests. Still missing notes cards for the research paper. Overall 38 percent.

Then math: Quiz grades are okay. Tests and homework are really hurting you. You seem to have some problems with dividing fractions. I'm available after school on Tuesdays and Thursdays for extra help if you want it. It's really hard to do well and keep up when you have thirteen absences already this year. Overall, you are at a 58 percent.

Depending on the student, you can see indifference, shame, or defiance rising. At this point, sometimes the parents are crying, sometimes the kid is crying. We keep a box of tissues on the table for these kinds of meetings, just in case.

Now it is my turn: You're missing such and such assignments, but you could make those up to get some more points. Test grades are such and such. Overall you are at a 67 percent ...

Through most of the meeting, I stare at my hands, unable to look the family in the eye. I wonder what they must be feeling and thinking, what other struggles they have in their lives, how meetings like this must add to those struggles, how many meetings like this they have been summoned to in the past, and why we keep holding them when I have never seen an improvement in the situation as a result in the five years I've been at the school.

Mostly, I'm ashamed to be there.

PRINCETON LEARNING COOPERATIVE IN PRINCETON, NEW JERSEY

November 2015, 8:35 a.m.

I meet with a potential new family from one of the local middle schools. They've just finished telling me about how hard school has been for their thirteen-year-old son, Mike. He's not doing well in any of his classes. The family is in turmoil, fighting night after night about getting homework done. They have had meeting after meeting with the school and nothing works. He is shutting down, losing interest in things he used to love. It's hard to get him out the door in the morning for school.

The parents' anxiety and fear for their son is overwhelming. They heard from a friend that PLC may be a solution to their school struggles, but they are worried that stepping off the traditional path is the wrong decision, with potentially catastrophic consequences.

Now it's my turn to speak. I address myself directly to Mike. "Many people don't know this, but you don't need to go to school to have a successful and meaningful life. In fact, you never have to set foot in a middle or high school again, unless you want to, and every option is still open to you—college, career, etc. You can leave all of the grades, tests, homework, and battles behind and focus on the things that you love to do on your own schedule. If you decide you want to join Princeton Learning Cooperative, we'll have mentors, classes, tutors, trips, workshops, help with finding volunteer opportunities, and a safe and welcoming community of teens and adults available on a totally voluntary basis. We're not going to force you to do anything. We'll provide the time, space, and support for you to figure out what you want in life, and then we'll help you get there."

This is almost certainly the only time an adult in Mike's life has told him these things. He doesn't say much, just responds with a couple of words here and there to direct questions, but he is listening and alert.

Meetings like this are by far the best part of my job. It feels like I am making a life-changing impact on Mike and his family, like I am helping to spread a little more light in a dark room. What I am doing on a daily basis matters and is valued.

We spend the next forty-five minutes talking about how all this is possible, covering how PLC works, and answering any questions or concerns they have about leaving school. Many times the young person starts the meeting slumped down in his or her chair thinking, *Mom is dragging me to another meeting with another school*, but is sitting upright and smiling by the end.

Mike nonchalantly says yes, he would like to stick around for the day to see what PLC is like. This is when many parents start crying. It has been so long since their son or daughter has smiled or said yes to anything.

We keep a box of tissues on the table for these kinds of meetings, just in case.

LARGE PUBLIC HIGH SCHOOL OUTSIDE PHILADELPHIA

May 2011, 4th period

I teach a current issues class to about twenty seniors. One of our topics is schools and alternative education. We do some calculations about their school careers: thirteen years, kindergarten through twelfth grade, about 1,260 hours of school each year not including homework, about $15,000 spent per student per year in our district, twenty students in the class. Grand totals: 327,600 hours spent in school and about $3.9 million dollars invested by the community in their educations.

I ask the class what they think of that. In the back, Maria raises her hand. "What a waste," she says. The other nineteen quickly murmur their agreement. I don't say anything but silently agree.

Not every student I teach thinks school is a waste, but a lot of them do. It makes me question all of the time and effort I put into this work. Could I be putting my energy into something with a greater purpose, meaning, and value to the young people I work with? How many of my students would spend time in my class or be interested in the things that I can offer them if it was all voluntary, if they didn't have to come unless they wanted to?

Maybe two out of twenty?

One?

I know what teachers often tell themselves about this and what I told myself about it too: *if I can just reach one student, then all the effort is worth it.*

Is it really? Is a 5 percent success rate really what I want for my life and my work? Shouldn't I find a way to have a bigger impact?

Sometimes I daydream about having twelve students, $180,000 for ten months, and no unreasonable restrictions on what we could do. Would the experience be better than school for the students? Would it be better for the adults?

PRINCETON LEARNING COOPERATIVE IN PRINCETON, NEW JERSEY

May 2014

PLC staff members are talking with a family whose fifteen-year-old son, Sean, joined about a month ago. He was a freshman at a local public high school. When we first met Sean, the situation the family described was not good. He thought school was a waste and felt that the things he was being asked to do didn't matter to him. He didn't see the relevance to his life down the road. He became increasingly frustrated and angry. Sean's social situation at school was not good either. He was starting to shut down, abandoning things he loved, retreating into his room, and pulling back from relationships with family, friends, and others.

This is not the path we want young people to be on.

We talk about how life is different now that he has left school. Sean's parents tell us how amazed they are at the differences they see and the possibilities that have opened up for their son. The teen is mostly quiet but looks up and participates in the meeting, which is new.

When he joined PLC, he expressed interest in a couple of pursuits—blacksmithing, HAM radio, conversational Russian, and guitar, among others. Not your typical stuff. When I taught social studies in school, if a student who was struggling in my class had come to me and said, "Mr. Hammon, I'm not really feeling this history stuff. What I would really like to do is learn more about HAM radio or learn to speak Russian," I would have said, "Sorry. Tough luck. There's really nothing I can do for you. We don't have any electives in those things. I can't really let you study that in social studies class because we have material to get through that you will be tested on at the end of the year and I want you to be able to pass. I don't really know anything about those topics myself. Maybe you can do some research during study hall or maybe in the evenings after your homework is done."

In any case, not something I was in a position to help, really.

At PLC, we can take teens' interests seriously and help them pursue them. We found the last remaining blacksmith in Trenton and helped set up an apprenticeship on Saturdays. We found the Princeton HAM radio club, and they had someone who was willing to come over and work with Sean an hour a week to get his license. We put out a call to our mailing list and found someone to do conversational Russian with him. He also joined a handful of PLC classes that were more traditional and continued his work at School of Rock playing guitar and bass. All of a sudden within a few weeks time, he went from feeling miserable and really disliking how he spent his time in school to having activities and interests that he felt were meaningful for his own life.

It is hard to describe how life-changing this can be for a teen and his family. Not everyone who leaves school and joins PLC has success stories like this, but it is definitely the rule and not the exception. As an educator, it feels amazing to be partners with young people and their families in such a deep and meaningful way.

LARGE PUBLIC HIGH SCHOOL OUTSIDE PHILADELPHIA

November 2009, Seventh Period Study Hall

I sit at the desk in the study hall I cover during seventh period. During this time, the ninth- through twelfth-grade students are not supposed to talk, use their cell phones, or sleep, according to school regulations. My basic philosophy on study hall goes like this: Look, I'm busy. I'm going to be sitting up here working. I don't really care what you do as long as it is at your seat and quiet enough that I don't have to look up. The students appreciate that stance and mostly sleep with their heads on desks with their hoodies up, listen to music on their iPods, or talk quietly with the person next to them. Some actually do homework.

Today, I take a break from grading a set of tests. I look toward the back of the long room, and there sits Brett—a sophomore who is on the baseball team and is a bit of trouble—looking back at me. On his desk in plain view is an empty iced tea bottle with a quarter of an inch of dark brown fluid in the bottom. He has a bulging lip. I sit there for a moment in disbelief, wondering if it is really possible that he is using tobacco in plain sight in study hall. I get up, walk to the back of the room, and ask him if he has a dip in. He says no. I ask him to stand up, and I see a round snuff tin–shaped bulge in his pocket.

Tobacco use on school grounds is a policy violation and must be reported. I confiscate the tea bottle, ask him to hand over the tin, and call down to the office to get coverage for my class while I take him down to the vice principal's office. I fill out the write-up sheet and turn the situation over to the vice principal. I'm not sure if the police were called, but he ends up getting a couple of days of in-school suspension and is suspended from the baseball team, which he loves and is likely one of the few bright spots in his life.

All the other staff members I tell the story to have basically the same reaction: man, how dumb can a kid be? At the time, I have the same reaction. It's not until later that I start to question the role I played in that interaction and think about what would really have been in the best interest of Brett.

PRINCETON LEARNING COOPERATIVE IN PRINCETON, NEW JERSEY

February 2013

Madison, one of our sixteen-year-old members, smokes. I'm her mentor, and her smoking starts to become somewhat of an issue. She comes back from walks reeking of smoke. She walks to the shopping center with other PLC members who don't smoke and is possibly starting to influence them. Parents who pick up and drop off their kids see her walk down the main road smoking, and I've started to get questions about it.

I bring it up in our mentoring meeting. She says she smokes to relieve stress. Her parents know about it but don't love it. I think one of them smokes as well. I don't need to tell Madison about the health effects of smoking; she knows all of that. She says she would like to quit. I share some of the difficulties her smoking is causing for the PLC community and for me personally, but mostly we talk about how much we care for her and want her to be healthy and her best self. We think about ways to stop smoking. She says that in the past eating sunflower seeds has helped because it gives her something to chew on and something to do with her hands. I also share some of my struggles to deal with my extreme caffeine addiction.

Later that week when I'm at the grocery store, I pick up an industrial-size bag of sunflower seeds and give them to her at our next meeting. She's touched by the gesture. We also talk about helping each other kick our habits. Let's do it together. I stop caffeine cold turkey and she stops smoking. When either of us feels the urge to indulge, we text the other person for support.

LIBERATED LEARNER MEMBER PROFILE
George Popham, Bay State Learning Center

I loved substitute teaching in high schools. The students recognized my enthusiasm for what I taught and that I was teaching them the way I had taught college students. Because I was so successful as a substitute, schools wanted to hire me. That's when I found out where the problems were. I wanted to engage the kids on an intellectual level, not play all the silly power games that seemed to be required, like arguing with students about whether or not they should take off their hats.

There were deeper problems as well. If I didn't want to teach a particular book or felt another book would be more relevant for the students, there was a whole process that I had to go through; I couldn't make decisions on my own about what to teach. Then there was the whole culture of test preparation where entire weeks got lost to this mindless trivia quiz-type practice that doesn't really teach any kind of deeper understanding of the material. Test prep doesn't lead to a broader intellectual life or any kind of real insight, and the kids hated it.

I felt that abiding by the rules that public schools required was harmful to the kids I was trying to teach, and I realized I couldn't do it. That was a really dark time because I was realizing that the career I had invested five years in was not going to work for me. I was actually depressed, but I did start thinking, *If I could start my own school, what would it look like?*

I looked into many things and tried to evolve some kind of business plan for myself, but I was stumbling around in the dark. One day, I was in western Massachusetts with a friend and happened to drive past North Star: Self Directed Learning for Teens. We pulled over, got some literature, and visited the website, and I knew instantly that North Star was what I was looking for. This was the model; this was the way to go. It turned out, that summer was the second Liberated Learners conference. We attended, and that was pretty critical because we had been at a pretty low point and going to the Liberated Learners conference just fueled me.

About thirteen months after that, we started with twenty-four kids at Bay State Learning Center. Since we opened, I've never looked at the clock, wondering when the day was going to end. Usually, the day ends before I'm ready for it to be over. When I get home, I'm exhausted, but it's the kind of exhaustion I haven't known since I was a graduate student. The whole day, you're engaged. I'm in the common room or I'm in class, and I'm constantly talking to students or advising them or just watching them and monitoring their relationships and seeing what the dynamics are like in the space. I'm working with other staff to figure out what kinds of things can we develop. All of this good stuff is just constantly cranking, all week long.

Then there's also the fact that I simply get to teach the way I want to teach. My enthusiasm for what I do is appealing to the kids, so there's a core group that really wants to work on the stuff I'm into. We have some big classes that are very much like the kind of college atmosphere I found so successful years ago. In addition to being teachers, we are also friends and advisors and mentors to our students. Our students rely on and value us.

Our theoretical ideas about how self-directed learning centers work didn't play out perfectly. None of this is simple. You have to pay attention to everything that's going on and manage the details, but in the important ways, it has worked. I'm not the adversary anymore. I get to be the teacher. I get to be the person who has things to offer rather than a person who brings the hammer down. When you change that dynamic, it's dramatic. I've never been this happy with a job in fifteen years.

2

What Are We Talking About?

In this book, I'll be talking a lot about self-directed learning, North Star, "the model," homeschooling, unschooling, and alternative education as opposed to traditional public and private schools. Let me take a moment to explain what all of this means and the basic philosophy before we get started.

Kenneth Danford and Joshua Hornick were eighth-grade teachers in Amherst, Massachusetts, in 1996. The process of traditional schooling and the effect it had on both their students' lives and their own made them disillusioned. Instead of excitement and enthusiasm in their students, they saw young people doing just enough to get by, not really caring about the things they were being asked to do, and in some cases literally being harmed by the stress and anxiety caused by the process of schooling. Kenneth and Joshua wanted to have noncoercive relationships with young people that were based on mutual trust and respect, relationships that would support young people in finding and pursuing the things in life they cared about. They also didn't want to be "in charge" of young people's learning in the sense of making sure certain things happened; they wanted to play the role of trusted advisor and mentor and help to make things possible.

Having some experience with homeschooling, Joshua recommended a book to Kenneth called *The Teenage Liberation Handbook: How to Quit School and Get a Real Life and Education* by Grace Llewellyn. For Kenneth, the book was a revelation. It described homeschooled children who did not go to school, who led meaningful and interesting lives learning about things they cared about, and who went on to college or work and generally turned out all right. Actually, better than just all right. This type of homeschooling, where the interests of the children are at the center of their experiences and families do not follow an externally designed curriculum or educational plan, is called "unschooling" or self-directed learning.

Before reading *The Teenage Liberation Handbook*, Kenneth had held many of the common misconceptions about homeschooling that the general population largely holds: it is only for ultra religious families, it isolates children from their peers, and it mostly consists of doing school at home, with the parents teaching algebra lessons at the kitchen table. This certainly describes some homeschooling families, but the community is wider and more diverse. They run the range from devoutly religious folks to aggressively atheistic families, from school at home programs purchasing standardized curriculum created by textbook companies to unschoolers who use no curriculum at all.

As Kenneth understood more about the possibilities of homeschooling, he started to see it as a way to help the kids he saw struggling in his classroom. What if all the kids in school just decided to learn independently, filed their homeschooling paperwork tomorrow, and led lives like those described in *The Teenage Liberation Handbook*? Kenneth and Joshua realized that while this was absolutely an option for every family, few families would have the confidence or feel the inclination to pull their children from school and take this path. It would require an organization and program to make the jump seem less scary and to provide the support necessary to make living and learning without school a viable and inspiring option to people in the community.

They considered the kinds of support that would be necessary to help families leave school successfully.

First, there had to be a home base, a headquarters where kids could come throughout the week. There had to be adults who could act as advisors and mentors to help young people and their families think about and take advantage of the possibilities this kind of life could offer. There also had to be some academic support happening at the center in the form of classes, activities, and tutoring. Nonacademic support would be good, such as help finding internships, volunteer opportunities, and jobs in the community as well as help with college admissions if that is where kids were headed. A safe, welcoming community of young people and other adults would support the social needs of teens. Families would get support from staff, who would help them file the homeschooling paperwork, explain the range of options and possibilities, and review the plans before the parents submitted them to the local school district.

All of this would have to be provided on a strictly voluntary and optional basis. Families and teens could access all, or none, of this support depending on their situations and goals.

North Star's genius insight was that families could use homeschooling law as the legal mechanism to remove themselves from the traditional school system and then have the freedom and flexibility to build the kind of life and education they wanted for themselves. North Star would be the support system to make it possible for any family that wanted to try. And in addition to improving the lives of young people, leaving teaching and working with teens in this way would also improve the lives of the adults who worked at North Star.

Before we move on, I'll try to make the concept of the program and what happens at self-directed learning centers like North Star and Princeton Learning Cooperative more concrete. There are local variations in the way each center operates (for example, some are open five days a week while others are open three or four), but the basic philosophy and DNA of each center is the same. I'll use Princeton Learning Cooperative as an example.

PLC operates from September through mid-June. We are open four days a week (Monday, Tuesday, Thursday, and Friday) from 8:45 a.m. to 3:15 p.m. We run classes and activities on Mondays, Tuesdays, and Thursdays. Our teen members and staff propose and organize trips and special workshops on Fridays when there are no scheduled classes. We close PLC on Wednesdays for practical and philosophical reasons. Practically, this is when the staff meets and has meetings with families or performs outreach to the local community. Philosophically, we want to structurally make the point to our members and their families that we are not a school and that they should be working toward making lives for themselves. So they should take Wednesdays to volunteer, work on projects, have jobs, or even sleep. Whatever it is, we want our teen members to start developing skills to manage their own lives and time.

We have roughly thirty teen members (we use this term instead of students as another way to separate us from schools) at any given time and three core staff members who work full-time and are paid. We typically also have a full-time apprentice who learns how to work in and potentially open a self-directed learning center down the road. The core staff's main responsibility and where we spend the majority of our time is in mentoring teens and working one-on-one with them. We each typically lead three to four classes per week as well. The majority of our classes and tutoring is carried out by twenty-five to thirty community volunteers, members' parents, or work-study college students from Princeton University. Our teen members even lead some of our activities.

Our classes typically meet once a week for an hour or two depending on the class and are not intended to be comparable to high school courses. They are intended to expose and inspire interest in various topics so teens can dig deeper if they have an interest. All of the classes and tutorials that happen at PLC are only on the calendar because a member wanted them or people were interested in joining something a staff member or volunteer offered to lead. At any given time at PLC, there might be three to four classes happening, a couple of mentoring meetings going on, a one-on-one math tutorial, and kids hanging out in the large common room chatting, playing games, watching videos on their computers, playing Frisbee outside, or walking to the shopping center for lunch. Once a week, we have an all-group meeting where we discuss upcoming issues in the PLC community, plan trips, make announcements, and take care of whatever business the groups needs to pay attention to. In the past, we have discussed how to use a new room that became available, how to deal with offensive language in the community, ways that we can be safe and welcoming for visitors, Intentional Inspiration (we show and discuss short videos that we feel are powerful), and recycling at PLC, among many other topics.

There are a lot of "school-ish" things that happen too (reading, writing, math, history, etc.), but we do not call ourselves a school because there is one critical difference: everything that happens at PLC is voluntary. This includes attending PLC and signing up for or continuing classes and tutorials. Members are free to come and go from the center throughout the day. There are no institutionally mandated tests or quizzes. We don't issue credits or diplomas. There are no grades or even grade levels in terms of ninth, tenth, eleventh, or twelfth grade. Our members range in age from twelve to nineteen and there may be young people of all of those ages in a particular class. At sixteen or seventeen, many of our members start utilizing community colleges to take classes in areas they are interested in or to start building credits toward transferring to four-year colleges.

We don't provide transportation or busing to or from PLC, so members get dropped off by their parents, carpool, ride their bikes, or walk. Transportation is sometimes an issue because many PLC members are coming from quite a distance, but generally families make it happen through a combination of carpooling and schedule rearranging. I'm sure some families see the distance and lack of transportation and never get in touch with us because it is just not a possibility.

PLC does not have organized sports teams, although many of our members play on community teams or play pickup games. School districts in New Jersey have the discretion to allow homeschoolers to play on school teams and participate in afterschool activities, but many districts do not allow it. In Pennsylvania, where we also operate the Bucks Learning Cooperative, the homeschooling law requires school districts to allow homeschoolers to participate in extracurricular activities. The trade-off in Pennsylvania and some other states is that with this increased access to school resources comes greater regulation of homeschooling. Homeschoolers in Pennsylvania need to submit a curriculum plan to the district and also have a certified teacher sign off on a portfolio of work at the end of the year, among other requirements. Even with this increased regulation, the legal aspects of homeschooling are simple and compliance is easy.

We don't have the social rituals of high school such as prom or homecoming, but our members' friends may invite them to their school's prom or they can attend the New Jersey homeschooling prom.

The community aspects of PLC are one of the critical components of what we do. We constantly talk about how we want PLC to be a safe and welcoming place for everyone. We work very hard to promote mutual understanding among members and mediate conflicts when they arise, though they are rare.

If you were to walk into PLC's common room on any random Tuesday afternoon, you would find a group of happy, smiling, laughing teens at ease in their situations, which is not what my fifth-period US History class looked like when I was a teacher. We actually have what we call "Reverse Snow Day Syndrome." When I was a teacher and there was a snow day or we were otherwise closed, the kids cheered and hollered. At PLC, we have the opposite reaction: our kids complain about us being closed on Wednesdays, and when we have a snow day, they are disappointed. I can't tell you how refreshing and meaningful that is to me as an educator—students who actually want and value what we can provide them.

Taking a longer and more historical look at learning, we see an obvious fact that is largely ignored today: schooling and learning are not the same thing. Sometimes learning does happen in school, but not always and not for every kid. The system of compulsory education we have today with age segregated levels, standardized curriculum, textbooks, periods separated by bells, grades, tests, quizzes, credits, diplomas, etc., is a fairly recent development if you consider the whole of human history. It has actually only been around for one hundred and fifty years or so—a blink of the eye. And it is definitely showing its age.

How many of us, if we closed our eyes and tried to imagine the best way to support young people's learning and growth, would imagine something even remotely close to the system that we have in place today?

The truth is that all people, including teens and children, learn new things all the time in all kinds of places and in all kinds of ways. It is not necessary to huddle everyone into a building for seven hours a day, segregate them by age and ability, and have standardized curriculum in order for learning to happen. That is just one way of organizing the education of children. So the traditional model of schooling should not be considered the starting point for any discussion of learning, but simply as one option among many. We tell families who are interested in joining PLC all the time that once you step out of the traditional model and start looking around, you'll be amazed at all the resources and opportunities available to young people who do not go to school. Our role as adult educators needs to change from expert dispensers of information to guides, facilitators, and mentors for young people as they explore the world and figure out their roles in it.

LIBERATED LEARNERS MEMBER PROFILE

Abby Karos, Compass Centre for Self-Directed Learning

In my early twenties, I knew that I wanted to teach, but I also knew that I didn't want to teach in a traditional setting. Through the National Coalition of Alternative Community Schools, you could do a year-long internship and then get an alternative certification. I interned for a year at a school in Ithaca, New York. It was a great experience, but then I moved to Canada and this alternative certification meant nothing. So the years went by and I did other things, but I kept up with what was happening in the alternative education world. I would go to the Alternative Education Resource Organization conferences each year, and at one of those conferences I heard Kenneth Danford and teens from North Star give a presentation. That just seemed perfect for what I wanted to do. So that was the beginning of my interest in this model.

During this period, while I was keeping up with the alternative education world, I taught at a private school in Montreal, I taught university, I taught various ages including little kids, and then after I moved to Ottawa I eventually got my regular teaching certification. It was purely just for that piece of paper. I thought it would give me a bit more credibility with some families and certainly with the school board, and that has proved to be true.

When I was teaching at the private school in Montreal, I really liked working with the kids, even though the school ran counter to every education belief that I hold dear. At times I clashed with some of the other teachers, and there was a lot of homophobia there (I could see how they were talking about some of the kids who were gay), so all of that made it a negative experience. In spite of that, though, I really enjoyed teaching the kids.

My interest in education was about enjoying intellectual pursuits, and I knew that I preferred working with teenagers because with younger kids you can't really go where you want to go intellectually in the same way. After seeing the North Star panel at the conference, I wanted to open my own center, and I attended the North Star replication workshop two years in a row. At that time, I didn't yet have a codirector, and the idea of starting completely on my own was a little daunting. At the second replication conference, Ken put me in touch with Andre Morison, a former intern at North Star who was planning to move back to Canada. Things moved pretty quickly from there. We had maybe three months to start everything up. We got a website, we brought Ken and a group of North Star teens up for an information night, and we opened in January of 2013.

There's certainly a lot to juggle in running Compass. Especially with a small center starting out, a lot can depend on the membership that you have at any given time. We have a younger cohort this year, so the things that we're discussing in advising meetings are very different than what we'd be discussing with sixteen- and seventeen-year-olds. Many of these younger members are in the beginning stages of the process of being in charge of their own educations. Even if they are coming from a homeschooling background, they're still feeling like their parents are more in charge of their education than they are at this point. I can go along for a while in the daily routine and not think too much about the broader implications of what we're doing, and then something will happen to remind me. We'll find an amazing opportunity for a teen to work with a local artist and put on his or her own art show, or a new teen will come in and it will be so amazing for him or her to realize that this option exists for teens to have this much control over their educations, or we'll be on a panel at a conference and people will be so amazed at what we're doing.

It's always powerful when we meet interested community members who are energized just by hearing that this exists or when we have a meeting with a new family. Often, after we've met with the teen and the parents, the teen will go out and chat with some of the other kids and just get a feel for the space, and I can't even tell you how many times we've had a parent then completely break down in tears because it's been so hard up to that point. It's that moment when you realize how amazing it is, what you're doing, that there is this space where learning can be joyful and relationships can be so authentic. At Compass, we adults get grumpy about the teens' muddy boots or them not hanging up their coats, but when that happens, it's just me being another person who's annoyed, not me coming down from this place on high as an authority figure. There's no threat being held over them. They know that and I know that. As much as I enjoyed the relationships with the kids when I was teaching in school, at the end of the day I still had all the power, and working as a mentor or support person in the way we can at Compass really allows for a very different kind of relationship.

As terrifying as it seems before you do it, it's exciting to realize that you can take a risk and do something like we have done with Compass. Andre and I have made tons of mistakes, and we talk a lot about what we could have done differently with this event or that meeting with a family. Just that learning curve is so huge and exciting. It's immensely rewarding to know that through Compass we're making such a huge difference in the lives of these teens. It's basically the things that you hope for before you go into teaching. I don't have an administration that I'm battling against or a teaching staff in which our values are so different that it makes my whole work environment unpleasant.

3

Teaching

I come from a family of teachers. My dad is a retired teacher, my wife is a teacher, my mother-in-law is a retired teacher, my mom is a secretary at a school, a few of my aunts were teachers, a couple of my cousins are teachers, most of my friends are teachers, and I spent eleven years working as a teacher. I think it is fair to say that for my first thirty years of life a lot of my time was spent in school, from a kid hanging around my parents to a student and then as a teacher.

This was fine by me.

I loved hanging around my parents' school (the school I attended for first through eighth grade) playing in the gym, helping my mom sort and staple packets of paper, helping other teachers get their rooms ready, and just generally goofing around. I liked being a student. School worked for me. I got along with teachers and other kids, I did well academically, and I was in all sorts of sports and clubs. By all normal measurements, I thrived in school.

I remember vaguely deciding that I wanted to be a teacher like my dad in the seventh grade. Then I remember really admiring my eleventh-grade AP US History teacher. I don't remember all of the details that led me down the path to a teaching profession, but it was sufficiently clear to everyone that I was voted "most likely to return to Napoleon High School as a teacher" in our senior year student newspaper. There is a picture of me and Mr. Inselman holding up an AP history book out there somewhere. If you would have asked me as a high school senior why I wanted to become a teacher, I really wouldn't have been able to give you a good answer other than it just seemed normal to me, having been around the profession my whole life. In much the same way as if you asked me why I was going to college after high school, I really wouldn't have been able to give you a good answer; it just seemed like the thing you did next, like thirteenth grade.

I enrolled at Miami University in Oxford, Ohio, as a secondary social studies education major with history and political science minors, mostly because my older sister went there and because I heard they had a good education program.

At Miami I was confronted with a level of wealth inequality that was shocking to me, having come from a small farm town in Ohio where everyone was basically in the same boat—not really wealthy. I started meeting very rich people coming from the suburbs of Cleveland, Chicago, Columbus, and Cincinnati. Hearing about the trips they went on, the experiences they had, the people they knew, and the things they owned kind of blew my mind. Also during my freshman year, I had to do a school observation for one of my education classes and I saw a very poor school in Cincinnati where I'm sure most of the students were on free or reduced lunch. The school didn't have enough money to get copier paper. So this juxtaposition of wealth and poverty really started me thinking and began to give shape to a more adult sense of why I wanted to go into teaching. I wanted to help save disadvantaged kids, and by extension the world, through education.

Under the influence of my freshman year economics professor (and if we are being honest, the liner notes for Radiohead's *Airbag* EP), I started getting into politics and read anything I could get my hands on. I had never been a huge reader, but I started just roaming around the library, taking out books, and devouring them. I would usually have five to ten with me at all times, mostly on politics, history, and economics. This was the first time I had an intellectual life of my own as opposed to just doing what my teachers asked of me. I remember the distinct feeling that my classes in college were getting in the way of my actual learning. And in fact, all of the things that I remember most from college and that meant the most to me came from this self-pursuit of knowledge.

It was exciting and gratifying.

This study of society and economics gave shape to my understanding of inequality in the US and what my role as a teacher could be to challenge that, help young people change their situations, and lead to a more fair and equal society. I was now on a mission to rid the world of evil, and I was going to do it through the only vehicle I knew—school.

I did part of my student teaching at Aiken High School in Cincinnati, which is an inner-city school that had a lot of problems. My cooperating teacher was not very good, and not much happened in his classroom. In fact, I remember only actually teaching maybe one or two days during my eight weeks there, but it gave me a lot of time to talk to and interact with kids from very poor Cincinnati neighborhoods. It also started to break down my conception of the meaning, purpose, and usefulness of school. I had always thought of school as good, empowering, useful, but now I was interacting with kids who did not see it that way. To many of the kids there, school was something they were forced to do. To them, it was just a whole bunch of nonsense that had little to do with their lives or futures and the sooner they could stop going, the better. This belief was evidenced by the massive dropout rate and the fact that attendance hovered around 60 percent each day and it was never the same 60 percent.

I remember one student who, when asked to stand and say the Pledge of Allegiance, replied, "Man, fuck America." I remember another student who, when we were passing out a test, told me he wasn't going to take it. I thought maybe he wasn't feeling well or that he wanted to take it at another time, but no. He just wasn't going to take it, ever. This blew my mind. "What about your grades? What about passing the class? What about your future? What about simply doing what you are told in school?"

None of this was part of his calculation. He didn't say it out of malice or anger; he just wasn't going to play the game that day. I don't know if it was courage or folly on his part, but I would have never in a million years done something like that in school or knew anyone growing up who would have done that. It put a chink in my myth that school served everyone and had the power to improve lives. Obviously not for this kid at this point in his life. Maybe these kids had already figured something out that I hadn't. Down the road, I decided I couldn't play the game anymore as well.

At some point late in my college career or maybe just after I graduated, I came across *The Teenage Liberation Handbook*. One of the political writers I knew was into youth liberation and had mentioned the book. I read it and I don't think it had much of an impact on me the first time around. It was interesting but so outside my mental map of the world at the time that it didn't register.

Leave school? Preposterous! School was the path to changing the world. It was the force for good.

After I graduated and got my teaching license, I started applying for jobs. I was going to save the world, so I applied where I thought I was needed most—the inner city. I applied to Columbus Public, Cleveland Public, Chicago Public, Philadelphia Public (my eventual wife and I met in college, and she was from the Philly area), and Cincinnati Public.

I never heard from any of them.

I applied to a bunch of schools all over Ohio and had a bunch of interviews but only one job offer. It was at a small religious school in Toledo where I would have six different classes to teach and very little pay. I declined. Instead I moved back in with my parents and was a substitute teacher, mostly at my old high school. Since I was in the building almost every day and helped out as a tennis coach, I got to know many of the students there.

As was true for most of my career, for whatever reason, I tended to get along best and have the best relationships with kids who didn't like school.

There was one kid in particular that year at Napoleon High School who I interacted with a lot. I don't remember his name, but he was all punked out—leather, metal spikes, huge spiky blue mohawk. A very genuine, very nice kid. We somehow got on the topic of him not liking school that much, and very innocently, I suggested that I could loan him my copy of *The Teenage Liberation Handbook*. I was in a very intellectual mode at that time, with lots of ideas and not a lot of action. Sure the book talked about leaving school, but who would actually do that just because he or she read a book? To me it was an interesting idea but certainly not a guide to practical action.

So there I was, a teacher, giving a student *The Teenage Liberation Handbook: How to Quit School and Get a Real Life and Education.*

I'm not sure exactly what I expected was going to happen, but I saw him a couple of weeks later. He handed me the book back, thanked me for letting him borrow it, and told me he was dropping out of school.

I never saw him again.

These days I make my living letting teenagers and their families know that it is okay to leave school and that teenagers are not throwing their lives away or closing any doors, but I was not quite there yet in my teaching career. So my first reaction was "Holy shit! Did I just destroy this child's life?" Looking back now, I am in awe of his courage and will to act to make his life better, but at the time it shocked me.

The longer I stayed in my hometown, living with my parents and substitute teaching, the more I realized I needed to get out of there. In the meantime, my girlfriend had gotten a job teaching outside Philadelphia, so I decided to move out there to be closer to her and try my luck in a new place. No job, no money, no prospects. I had a car, an apartment, enough money for the first month's rent, and also the support of my family and girlfriend. I started applying for jobs everywhere (including the Guitar Center, Barnes and Noble, and Burger King) and didn't hear back from any of them. Just as the summer was about to end, I got a call from the school where my girlfriend, Kerry, worked. Their social studies department chair had left suddenly to take another position. They were in need of a social studies teacher quickly because school started soon, and they had heard from Kerry that I was moving to the area. So without applying, I was officially employed for the first time as a full-time teacher.

It was fairly ironic that after applying to teach in some of the toughest areas in the country, my first job was in a private all-girls Catholic high school in one of the wealthiest suburbs of Philadelphia. I was to teach American History, US Government, and Sociology. There was no curriculum, no real direction on what to do, and rooms they had scrounged together in a building on campus away from the main building. Perfect! I basically had total freedom to do whatever I wanted in regard to teaching, and I threw myself into the work.

I imagined a scene from *Dead Poets Society*. I was going to be the bearer of the torch of knowledge, leading my charges up the mountain of enlightenment to the pinnacle of truth and justice. My students would be just as enthusiastic for this quest as I was: "Yes, captain my captain! Show us the way!"

Instead what I mostly got were uninterested stares and questions like "Is this going to be on the test?" or "Why do we have to read this much?" and even "How big can the margins be on this paper?" Certainly there were some kids who really got what I was trying to do, loved the class, and were moved by the experience, but certainly not the majority. I remember one particularly gratifying experience when I had students who were not on my rolls cutting classes to come with their friends to my class and hear me rail against the reasons being given for war on the eve of the second Iraq war in 2003.

At first, I thought the malaise was my fault, so I tried harder. I did innovative things in class. I tried to make everything more relevant to today and to their own lives. We took trips and read interesting books after I ditched the textbooks, but that still didn't do it. It was about as ideal of a situation I could imagine for practicing the craft of teaching: total freedom in terms of curriculum, with the most disruptive discipline problem being when students weren't wearing their uniforms to specifications. But the end result was not what I imagined in my young, idealistic mind about the power and possibility of school and education. Sure, some of the kids would say that being in my class changed their lives forever, and many would say that I was their favorite teacher, but the lesson I took away from those early years was that not everyone experienced school like I had. For many of my students, school was not a quest for knowledge or improving themselves. It was basically being in a place they didn't want to be, being made to do things they didn't want to do and would never do if they had a real choice. For them, school was simply something to get through. That was all.

In fact, some of the kids I worked with didn't see high school as four years of opportunity for growth. Instead, they looked at it like a four-year prison sentence. Well, this was news to me, and I really started to question the value school and my role in the system had in the lives of my students. Discontent was brewing. Making kids who didn't want to be there do things they didn't want to do is not a pleasant way to go through life and was certainly not why I went into teaching in the first place.

Meanwhile, my wife at this point had left the school we both taught at to take a job at one of the big suburban public schools in the area. Midway through my third year of teaching, a position opened up in the same school district in social studies. We knew some people who would be involved in the hiring process, so I applied and got the job. With a salary schedule that topped out at over $100,000 a year, full and free health benefits, and essentially a job for life unless I quit or committed serious crimes, walking into a full contract in this school district was like hitting the teacher lottery. Hundreds of people applied for each open position. So midway through the year, I went from teaching juniors and seniors on Friday to teaching seventh graders on Monday. It was an interesting change, and I threw myself into the work.

There were some changes: more curricular requirements to follow, more discipline issues to deal with, and more horrible staff development days to sit through. But the essential problems persisted, and I realized more and more that they were systemic. No amount of tinkering around the edges was going to solve the problem of school for many of the kids I worked with. I continued to do what I considered innovative things, and many of my students would say mine was their favorite class, but it became more and more clear to me that I needed to get out.

I had gotten into teaching to help kids grow, see bigger and more opportunities, imagine possibilities, and be turned on to life, but instead I saw the opposite happening for many of my students, and I didn't want to be part of a system that was doing that to kids.

Along the way, young people I worked with showed me the ways school didn't work for them: The kid who had such terrible anxiety about school that the only way he could get himself into the day was to come up to my room before school and play guitar with me for a while. The kid who was crazy smart but failing all of his classes (I think he had a 2 percent in my class) because he refused to do any of the work; meanwhile he was asking me if I had any books about anarchy and carried around a dictionary to look up the words he didn't know in Thoreau's "On Civil Disobedience." The kid who was mercilessly picked on because he had a streak of white running through his dark brown hair. The kid who loved computer programming and deep thinking but was failing his other social studies class because he didn't keep his binder organized the way the teacher wanted. All of these great kids and a system that wasn't working for them. I wanted a different way to work with them, a different relationship.

It was during this timeframe (2005–2006) when things were at their worst. I was miserable. I hated what I did on a daily basis, and I just knew at the most fundamental level that I needed to get out if I was going to survive intact. One small problem: if you are a teacher but hate teaching in schools, what exactly are you supposed to do? It wasn't like I had skills or training in any other area. I was pretty desperate. I would Google things like "jobs for teachers who don't like teaching." Around this time, I started to reread *The Teenage Liberation Handbook*, which had been sitting on my bookshelf. As I read, I came across maybe a sentence or two mention of a place called Pathfinder that was started by two middle school teachers. For whatever reason, this description intrigued me enough at the time to try to find them online. I did a little digging and eventually put together that Pathfinder had changed its name to North Star, and I found their website.

I still remember this night distinctly. It was maybe a Wednesday at 10 p.m., and I was just dreading going to school the next day. I started to read the North Star website, and as I began to understand what they did and how they worked with kids, I became more and more excited. When I finally got it, it was like one of those eureka moments. I literally started jumping up and down in my office and did a little Irish jig around the room. I was so overjoyed.

This was the answer to my prayers. The ray of hope in an otherwise pretty dark existence.

I immediately wrote a desperate e-mail to Kenneth. It basically said: "Hi, Kenneth. I'm a teacher outside of Philadelphia, and I hate teaching. Help!" To Kenneth's eternal credit, he replied right away, and kindly. He invited me to come visit North Star at some point and also let me know about their first ever replication conference, which they were holding that summer to let people know how the model worked and how they could bring something like North Star to their communities.

Perfect! I was in.

4

Creating the Foundation

I finally knew what I wanted to do, and North Star was it. I started reading and rereading everything on North Star's website, especially the teen and parent testimonials. I asked Kenneth to send me a complete set of their past newsletters. I asked for a copy of their documentary. I became totally immersed in anything North Star had created.

Of course, coming from a traditional background I had lots of questions about how this works: How can kids move forward without a high school diploma? Isn't there some value in a traditional education that these kids would be missing out on? What about sports and clubs? What if kids do nothing but play video games? What if they decided to go for a walk and smoke pot?

I had a million questions, but I was so intrigued that I wanted to learn everything Kenneth and North Star had to offer.

So Kerry and I planned a trip to Boston over spring break in 2007 with a scheduled stop in Hadley, Massachusetts to meet Kenneth and visit North Star. I don't remember much about that first meeting. I remember sitting on couches in the common room. I remember meeting Kenneth and Susannah Sheffer and Catherine Gobron briefly. I remember the disgustingly moist carpets at the local Howard Johnson hotel. And I remember coming away absolutely thrilled. I signed up for the summer conference.

The replication conference was amazing and opened up this new world to me. There were five participants from all over the country, and Kenneth and Joshua Hornick, cofounder of North Star, took the group through the basics of how the North Star model worked. We talked a lot about how the educational model worked, working with teens and parents, how the volunteers and work study students played a part, and the more practical aspects of their work. They also laid out how the business and financial side of the model worked.

This was all new to me. I had always held frontline worker jobs throughout my life, so I had never been exposed to how budgets work, how boards and committees work, or how to deal with the IRS and other government agencies. It all seemed like an exciting challenge. I left that weekend totally convinced that this was what I wanted to do with my life, and I committed myself to working to open my own North Star center. As history would play out, the Princeton Learning Cooperative didn't open until 2010, three full years after the replication conference. I didn't quit my job and start working at PLC until 2011.

So what happened during those years?

One of my most important takeaways from the conference was that you should not try to start a North Star model center by yourself. The workload can be crushing at times, the types and variety of the work require a whole host of skills that really only a team could supply, and the risk of burnout is huge. So one of my first tasks when I came back home was to start finding partners. I didn't have anyone particular in mind. It was going to be a search from scratch. So I went about it in what seemed to me the most reasonable way. I thought I should find organizations in the area and get involved through volunteering. I hoped that by being active in my community I would meet people who resonated with the North Star mission and wanted to be partners.

There were a lot of things I was doing during this time that in hindsight look like a really well-planned process to gather the skills and experiences necessary to open the Princeton Learning Cooperative, but in reality it was nothing of the sort. I was doing things that I found interesting and tried to be open to all kinds of experiences. It is very much like the Steve Jobs commencement address at Stanford: You can't connect the dots moving forward; you can only do it looking backward.

So I started doing a bunch of seemingly random things that were eventually critical to my learning and development and my ability to contribute to the launch and growth of PLC. One of the first things I did was contact a local farm not too far from my house called Snipes Farm. They advertised educational programs, and I saw a sign for a Greenpeace event they were holding. I thought, *These are people I should get to know.*

So I e-mailed them to set up a meeting with Jonathan Snipes and learned that they had just created a nonprofit organization to do organic farming and educational programs in the community. I started volunteering for their Community Supported Agriculture program and from there got more and more involved with the work of the organization. The people at Snipes are some of the nicest people I have ever met, and I really love the work they do. Eventually they invited me to be on the board. It was the first time I had ever done something like that. I eventually held executive positions in the organization like treasurer and secretary. I learned so much being on the board, including budgeting, how nonprofits work, fundraising, how to lead an organization, the importance of organization and coordination … the list could go on and on. The people at Snipes would also play a much more direct role in bringing PLC together later.

I had also been volunteering in some pretty rough neighborhoods in North Philadelphia, doing sports programs with kids. I started a program called The Bridge to offer microfunding to kids from the neighborhood to go to college or get an apartment and start work. The program didn't get very far, but from leading that I learned how to run a meeting, talk to people about donating money, set up rudimentary websites, etc.

The people I met through this volunteer activity asked me to fill in as director at a summer camp for kids that one of the churches ran. So I did, and I learned about managing a group of about thirty kids, collecting payments, keeping records, scheduling, and managing a staff.

I started researching alternative education centers in my area and set up a meeting with Peter Bergson from Open Connections and attended one of their events to learn about homeschooling law in Pennsylvania and the whole world of alternative education. Through this search, I found and spoke with Amy Childs, who is an unschooling advocate in Philadelphia. She is well connected in the alternative education world. Amy would play an important role in PLC coming together as well.

My father-in-law owned a digital publishing company. He had booths at trade shows in Washington, D.C., and New York City, and he asked me to help run the tables. So I learned how to succinctly explain new concepts to total strangers in a short period of time and also how to follow up with the new contacts we made. I set up a Limited Liability Company (LLC) to run my tutoring money through and learned about incorporation, dealing with the state, and designing flyers and business cards.

It was a bunch of seemingly disconnected and incongruous activities, but now looking back at them, I realize I learned critical skills that served me well as we launched PLC: nonprofits, organizing, promotion, the business side of things, thinking about mission and vision, articulating what we were doing, and money. The list could go on and on.

During this time, I knew I wanted to create something like North Star, but I was still stuck teaching. And it didn't get any better. The thing that really gave me hope and kept my spirits up was North Star and the beautiful example they gave to the world. I would pour over their website almost daily for any updates or new material they published. The blog Catherine Gobron wrote was especially inspiring. I would show the North Star documentary to my seventh-grade classes and discuss it with the kids. "Okay, so who would like to leave school?" I would ask. It's amazing I didn't get fired. I suppose no one in the school administration was paying attention.

In some ways I felt like a spy. I didn't really tell anyone what I was up to. Not because I thought I would get in trouble but because I wasn't sure people would understand and it could lead to a lot of awkward conversations. So by day I was part of the system, faithfully plodding away, but by night I was planning my escape.

In 2009, I moved from the middle school where I worked to the large high school in the district where Kerry was also working. I hoped that maybe going back to the high school level would make teaching a bit more tolerable.

Nope.

Within about a week it became abundantly clear to me, as it must to young people who don't like middle school and hope that high school will be so much better, that it was going to be the same old thing. It was nice that I had the opportunity to teach a lot of my former students from middle school again in high school. It was also nice to work in the same building as Kerry again, and a lot of the people teaching in the social studies department were fun, but I was still miserable.

For me, caffeine is a serious mood enhancer, and I guzzled buckets of it every day just to make it through. Even my teaching, which I thought used to be good and innovative, slowly made the slide back to routine and boring as the subtle influence of district curriculum, state standards, department-wide midterms and finals, textbooks, and conversations about "where I was" in the curriculum started to take their toll.

Then it started to happen. In the winter of 2009, my prayers were answered in the form of Paul Scutt. Paul was a mutual friend of the Snipes family from Snipes Farm where I served on the board. Paul was the beekeeper for the farm as well as a disgruntled math teacher at one of the local private schools. Jonathan Snipes knew that neither Paul nor I liked teaching and suggested I reach out to Paul and have a conversation. So I called him up and left a message. He called me back and we set up a time to meet over coffee. This was the first meeting of what would eventually become the Princeton Learning Cooperative.

Paul brought along Martin Smith, who taught at the school Paul worked at, and the three of us formed the nucleus of the steering committee that would start to build the ideas, structures, and team behind PLC. I don't remember much about that first meeting other than that it was productive. I liked Paul and Martin very much, and I was excited. We agreed to meet again. Paul and Martin had not heard of North Star at this point, but they were very familiar with some of the other alternative education models like democratic free schools, Montessori, Waldorf, and Sudbury. Paul was also very interested in project-based learning and outdoor education. His wife, Jane Fremon, was founder and director of the Princeton Friends School, which is a very successful progressive K–8 Quaker school. PLC would draw a lot of our early support from folks connected to the PFS community.

I learned in bits and pieces about Paul over the years, and he has a fascinating life story: Born and raised in East Africa to British parents, he had at various times been a teacher, computer scientist, and ship engineer. He climbed mountains, was a skilled woodworker, fixed motorcycles, and was a beekeeper.

We decided we wanted to create something, some kind of alternative to traditional schooling, but we did not have a group consensus on what that would be. I was, of course, very interested to create something based on the North Star model, but it was an open question at this point.

The best way forward seemed to be to assemble anyone we knew who was involved in education as well as friends, community members, parents, former students, etc., to brainstorm ideas about what would be best for young people's education and growth and what kinds of structures and programs could be put in place to support that.

We ended up holding a large group meeting at Paul's house and invited everyone we could think of. It ended up attracting about thirty people, some of whom would play a large part in the founding of PLC, particularly Ajay Dravid, who would be a founder and was a friend of Paul's, and Matthew Shelley, a former student of Paul's who would design our logo, build our first website, and eventually apprentice at PLC.

That first meeting was great. A lot of really good ideas came out of it. No decisions were made about what we were going to build, but I presented a short thing about North Star and we started talking about other inspiring models the group knew of. We started to build our tribe of supporters and get the word out in the community that something was brewing. We also decided to meet again. Martin, Paul, and I would do the planning and logistics for the group.

Fewer people attended the second meeting, but we started to get more specific about what we wanted in our project, and the commitment level of the people who came was higher. At our third meeting, it became clear who was going to be the most involved—Ajay, Martin, Paul, and me—and that this group was fairly serious about creating something. But something was still not settled.

At this point, it was early spring of 2010. I was committed to the North Star model. If our group had decided to create a charter school, a private school, or really any school at all, I would have declined to participate. If I was going to work in a school and be miserable making kids do things they didn't want to do, I made a lot more money at my current school, plus there are plenty of schools for families to choose from. Simply making another one, no matter how cool, was not particularly inspiring to me. It was either North Star or bust.

The four eventual founders of PLC continued to meet throughout the spring. The main topic of conversation was what exactly we planned to create. My recollection of how those meetings went is pretty fuzzy. I remember making a chart comparing the different models on various aspects of learning: grades or no grades, mandatory attendance or not, curriculum or not, etc. Kenneth from North Star came down at some point for a weekend and talked to us all about the model. I remember the group having concerns about the financial model and if it could really work. In the end, we eventually decided as a group that the North Star model was most closely aligned with our sensibilities.

I remember distinctly the moment all of this became very real for me. Up to this point, we had been discussing plans and philosophy and hypotheticals. All very easy to give up on. In one of our meetings when it seemed we had reached a consensus on what we were going to build and had done as much planning as we knew to do at that point, Ajay said, "Okay. When are we going to open?"

It seemed like September 2011 made the most sense. Once that was decided and all of the discussion and thinking and planning was boiled down to a date on the calendar that I could look at and count down the days to, it became very concrete and real for me. The idea of quitting my job and being free of school, of having a conversation about quitting with Kerry, of starting something I had zero experience doing with zero guarantee of success and quite a bit of risk (at the time I had a large mortgage and a small child) became both exhilarating and terrifying.

As fate would have it, the timeline to start PLC got a big push forward. For various reasons Paul decided to leave his teaching position. So all of a sudden, we had a staff member available to run a pilot program in September of 2010. Instead of having fifteen months to organize and get ready to open, we now had a couple of months.

The race was on!

5

A Self-Directed Start-Up

What does it take to start a small education-based nonprofit? Quite a bit, it turns out. Incorporating, getting an EIN number, starting the IRS nonprofit status process, negotiating with insurance companies, securing space, building a functional team, getting a telephone, creating a website, figuring out payroll, health insurance, pricing, bookkeeping. Oh, and did I mention figuring out what in the hell we were doing? We also had to recruit paying members for this thing that no one had heard of and that we only had a fuzzy grasp of ourselves. (The main thrust of our argument was, "Pull your kid out of school. It will be fine.") And we had to accomplish all this before we opened for business day one. The word intense barely begins to describe it.

The long and short of it is that we pulled it off. We got enough of the pieces pulled together and opened for business in September 2010 in one little room in the Arts Council building in downtown Princeton. Our rent was $1,000 a month, and we had three full-time and two part-time teen members. Paul was the staff person there every day. I was the president of the board and did a lot of the administrative tasks like invoicing, bookkeeping, and dealing with the IRS while I continued to teach full-time at the high school.

Even to get to this small grand opening was quite an achievement. A couple of contributing elements were critical.

Paul had extensive ties to the Princeton area through his connection with Princeton Friends School. Many of our early members came to us because they knew Paul or me personally or knew someone we knew well and trusted us. Having connections in the community is huge. The larger culture tells families at every opportunity that children have to stay in school because it is the only way to have a successful life. So asking families to leave school and send their children and money to you is a really big leap. Knowing Paul and me personally and knowing we weren't crazy helped a lot in those early days.

The other thing that was really important was the makeup of the team we put together. We all brought different skills and strengths to the group. Paul was great at working with kids and forming relationships. I was happy to do the planning, organizing, and administrative work. Ajay had experience working in established businesses and knew how the world of money worked. Martin was good at group process and asking clarifying questions about what and how we were doing things. We could also draw on connections with folks who volunteered to help us set up our first website and brochure. If we had formed a team of just people who wanted to work directly with teens or a team of people who were only good at filling out IRS forms, it wouldn't have worked. We needed balance, and we had it.

The first year, or pilot program, was instructive and fantastic in a lot of ways. First, it was obvious that leaving school and doing self-directed learning had resulted in an immediate and dramatic improvement for our members who needed it most. So the educational model was solid. We also learned that the leap from "my kid is unhappy in school" to "I'm going to take my kid out of school" was a lot bigger than we had imagined. When I was teaching, I worked with dozens of kids a year who didn't really like school and would have benefited from this model. I had thought that once we started PLC, people would just flock to it. Not the case. For kids as well, not liking school and deciding to leave school are two totally different things, and there is a wide gap between them.

So the imperative, overarching takeaway was this: This is a good idea that many people will benefit from. We just need to figure out a way to keep the doors open long enough that enough people hear about it and join.

That was it. Any audience, any person we could get in front of and talk to about PLC, we were there: farmers markets, community festivals, flyers in all the local shops and libraries. Anyone, anywhere, anytime.

The phone was mostly silent. So much in fact that to this day I am like a trained rat. The ringtone of the PLC phone is burned into my psyche like a blazing fire. Any time that thing went off (and I could probably count the number of times on my fingers and toes during the first eighteen months we were open) some sort of chemical—adrenaline, dopamine, endorphins—flooded my body. I still get that ultimate rush when someone inquires about PLC.

We also learned rejection, failure, and improvement. We held a series of open houses and informational sessions during the first year, and around fifty families attended. Exactly zero of them joined. Part of the problem was that we were addressing educational philosophy and not what mattered most to the families—the well-being of their kids and how we could help them. We learned that lesson and got better at describing PLC and the benefits of joining in terms that addressed families' needs.

Also critical to the early and subsequent success of PLC was bringing Alison Snieckus into the organization. As PLC was starting, we reached out to Amy Childs, a homeschooling guru based in Philadelphia. She put out the word in the homeschooling networks that we were starting up. Alison was deeply involved in the homeschooling movement in New Jersey, having homeschooled both of her boys through high school. She also cofounded and ran an organization called E3. E3 offered a once-a-week gathering and self-directed learning opportunities for homeschooled teens. Alison knew about North Star and at one point had considered starting her own center, so she was very excited to learn about what we were proposing.

She got in touch with us, and I still remember our first phone conversation. I paced back and forth in my hallway upstairs, and it was just, "Yes, yes, yes." We were very much on the same wavelength educationally and philosophically. This was someone we needed to have involved. Shortly after PLC's founding, she joined the board and volunteered at PLC during the pilot year and the first year that I was on staff.

By far the best decision Paul and I ever made was to ask Alison to join the staff full-time during the 2011–2012 campaign. To be perfectly honest, Paul and I had known almost nothing about homeschooling and how to do it well when we started PLC, or how homeschoolers applied to college or got involved at community colleges, how to mentor teens, or really anything else. She enthusiastically came on full-time even though we couldn't pay her at first, and she brought absolutely critical knowledge, experience, and process to the group, showing once again how critical it is to build a team with the right mix of complementary skills and knowledge. It's pretty safe to say that PLC would not be where we are today—or maybe even be around at all—without Alison.

Alison's involvement also points to another key aspect of starting a self-directed learning center or, really, any other organization: people have to be in love with the mission.

PLC has been fortunate to attract and retain amazing people (even when we can't pay them enough or there doesn't seem to be any external reward for their involvement) because our *why* resonates so strongly with them. They want to be involved in an exciting and potentially revolutionary movement and want to do something meaningful. So, talking about the big reason you exist as opposed to how you teach math or art to kids is what will build the program.

The view of PLC at the end of that first pilot year was this: We made it through the first year. The doors stayed open. We had attracted seven members by the end of the year, three of whom were planning to continue with us the following year. We had started to get the name and concept out into the community. We had put a good team in place. Paul had done his financial "year of pain," that is, really low pay the first year someone comes on staff (we funded the start-up of PLC not with a large lump sum of money but through drastically reduced salaries). We had learned a lot about how not to describe our program. We had attracted one large donation of $10,000 from one of our early supporters. And we were excited about moving forward.

The plan was that I would quit my job in the summer of 2011 and join the PLC staff full-time for our second year. At the time, it seemed like a sensible and obvious move. Looking back, it seems absolutely insane. We had only a handful of paying members coming back, we were to guarantee Paul at least $40,000 before I saw any salary (my year of pain), I had a hefty mortgage and a two-year-old, and I would be leaving a stable, well-paying job that had full benefits.

The lesson I drew from that—and I think this is true about any important undertaking whether it is starting a business or having a child—is that there is no perfect time to do it. Waiting until "all your ducks are in a row" is a way to let fear and hesitation sound reasonable and like a good idea. The truth is, if you wait for everything to be just right before you act, you will never act.

Even though there were a million reasons that quitting my job was crazy, I had a lot of things that made it much easier. The first was my wife, Kerry, who supported me leaving my job. She not only gave her blessing, but the fact that she was still teaching at the high school where I taught meant she had a stable, high-paying job that offered good health benefits and made my risk taking not as risky. We had also saved some money (though not a lot), and we had zero credit card debt. So I could be pretty confident that even if everything fell apart, we would be okay and would not lose our house or put our family in serious financial danger.

That last year of teaching while we were running the pilot program was a flurry of activity. I taught all day and squeezed PLC work into every crack of time I could. I called in sick to every mind-numbing staff development day so I could work on PLC. I remember one nice spring day ditching a day of presentations on the latest blah, blah, blah at the high school and going up to Princeton to visit the pilot program and walk around downtown, hanging up flyers. It was such an incredible feeling. It felt like I had been let out of prison, walking around like a free man with the sun on my face. It was beautiful, and I wanted more of it.

I was so miserable at the high school. How miserable, you may be asking? On the first day of my last year of teaching I prayed as I was coming up the driveway that the building had blown up overnight so I would never have to walk in there again. And so it went, day after day.

By the last day of school, it hadn't been officially decided between Kerry and me that I wasn't coming back next year, but I was positive I was gone. I surreptitiously cleaned out almost all of my stuff from my work space, and as I walked out of the building that day, I turned around in the parking lot, gave a middle finger salute, executed a deep bow, and bid that life adieu.

I was mentally and emotionally done. Finished.

Kerry and I discussed me leaving over the summer. It was a hard conversation, but to her credit, she believed in me enough to agree. I had been making all sorts of financial contingency plans: We could borrow maybe from these people. I could substitute teach if things really fell apart. I could get a job here or there. A lot of people have asked me if it was scary to leave the security of my job to try this thing that was totally uncertain. It absolutely was.

A couple of things helped me past the fear. First, I had no doubt in my mind that it would work. North Star had made it happen, and I had a lot of confidence in my own ability to do the work necessary to make it work. The other thing was that though it was scary to leave, it was absolutely horrifying to think that I was going to spend the next thirty years of my life teaching. I was really afraid of what that would do to my spirit and well-being.

When it came time to actually resign in August 2011, I was surprised. I thought it would be this hugely momentous, dramatic event like you see in the movies, but I was so mentally checked out of teaching by that point and so locked into the work of building PLC that I barely noticed it. It was just an item on my to-do list that day: pick up flyers from the printers, make these phone calls, quit my job, meet with the insurance agent …

In August 2011, I was officially out.

I had become an entrepreneur, even though I didn't think of myself that way at the time and knew next to nothing about business or marketing or finance or really anything. I had entered my year of pain. I was guaranteed nothing by way of salary until all of our costs were covered and Paul had at least $40,000 going toward his salary. There is no greater motivator than that. I used to have a fear of getting up in front of people and talking, calling strangers on the phone, or initiating conversations. There is no faster way to get over those fears than imagining if I don't make this call, my daughter won't have anything to eat or if I don't reach out to people at this farmers market, we could eventually lose our house. We weren't quite that desperate as a family, but it was certainly in my mind.

And so that first year on staff was both exhilarating and terrifying. It involved getting in front of anyone who would listen to me talk about PLC and initiating hundreds of e-mails, calls, and conversations. Most of these efforts were met with indifference, feigned interest, or outright rejection, but steadily we got the word out. It was also a year of tremendous personal and professional growth for me.

To help with finances, my wife and I started cleaning the rooms and bathrooms of the office of the teachers union in which she was involved for $50 a pop on the weekends. There's nothing more romantic than scrubbing toilets to help fund your dream, right? I started buying all my clothes at Salvation Army. This is a bit of an exaggeration, but at one point early in that year I had paid more in parking tickets to the city of Princeton than I had made from working at PLC.

We kept fighting and scrapping, but membership numbers stayed flat. We started the year with seven, and we stayed there all that fall, maybe picking up a member or two around Thanksgiving and the holidays.

At some point, Alison suggested in a board meeting that we should create a series of public events to highlight our philosophy of education and what life can look like for young people without school. The idea was that for us to survive and thrive into the future, we would need to change the culture and thinking around education. Yes, brilliant! Did I mention PLC wouldn't be around without Alison? So we created Outside the Box, a series of public events to highlight the philosophy and work we do. One of these events proved critical to our growth. We put together a panel discussion with local alternative high schools and homeschooling options and our press release got picked up by one of the local papers. They did a story about the event itself and then reached out about doing a larger story just about PLC.

The article ended up on the front page of the local newspaper with a big picture of Paul and me and some of our members. The next open house we held was packed, and four or five new members joined shortly after. This was January or February 2012. Luckily, just after the article ran, we had moved into larger space or else we wouldn't have been able to accommodate all the new folks. We went from nine members to fourteen to twenty, and I believe we finished the year with twenty-two. It was hard to keep up with it.

I remember getting my first paycheck from PLC. It was a feeling like nothing else, even though it was only for $500. The money came from families that valued what we were offering and voluntarily gave us money. It felt like the first money I had ever really earned, and I was having a blast doing the work. With that first paycheck, I wanted to show gratitude to the people in my life who had supported me. I took Kerry and her parents out to dinner. Then Kenneth from North Star came down to visit, and we went out to dinner. I also gave some money to our fabulous babysitter, Julia, who we'd had to short since I quit my job.

I remember the first time someone we didn't know recommended us to a friend. Until that time all of the people we had worked with were in some way connected to Paul or me or someone in the organization. I asked one of our inquiries where they had heard about us, and they said the name of someone we had never heard of. We had become established in the community at this point, and people knew about us. That made it feel very real to me at the time. It also showed me that some of the seeds we had planted over the first eighteen months were starting to sprout. It was a gratifying feeling.

All of this success didn't come easily or without cost. The amount of time, effort, focus, stress, and strain it took to get to that point took its toll. Ask me what my hobbies were during this period. None. Ask me how I spent my free time. On PLC work. Ask me how often I was home or when I was home how focused I was on my family. Very little. PLC was an all-out obsession, and it took the very best parts of my time, focus, energy, and attention and left very little for anything else. As we have built the program and our team, I have worked very hard to have more balance, but at that time I didn't see any other way to make this thing work.

As of 2016, PLC is thriving. Our team has started a new center under the same nonprofit called Bucks Learning Cooperative in Langhorne, Pennsylvania, and we're in the planning stages of starting another center in Flemington, New Jersey, called Raritan Learning Cooperative. We feel like the tide of education is starting to turn more toward the types of ideas we have been promoting for the past six years. PLC is a very different place than it was during the first couple of years, with more members, more staff, and more volunteers. But those early years of struggle were amazing and the most important in my life.

We learned a lot of lessons in the start-up phase of PLC. These are the ones that stand out the most:

1. It was absolutely critical to have the help of a mentor and people who knew what they were doing. In our case, this was Kenneth, Catherine, Susannah, et al. from North Star. They shared materials, served as an example of the model working for families, and coached us on how to deal with particular situations that arose. We may have been able to create PLC without them, but it would have been very slow going, and we would have made a lot more mistakes. This consulting and mentoring work is now done by Liberated Learners which is described in chapter 6.

2. Putting together a great team is crucial. Doing this alone or with a team that does not function well together would be a disaster. PLC was fortunate to assemble a team with deep complementary skills and experiences.

3. You have to be hooked into the local community. Almost all our early members and financial supporters were people who knew us directly. Being integrated into local organizations and people who are natural allies to this type of learning center is critical to getting the word out and attracting families.

4. Hard work is a requirement, along with many, many, many, many hours. This work can't just be a job to the founders; it needs to be a mission. Starting a center like this is not a part-time job or a side project.

5. While many aspects of PLC's start-up may seem like serendipity, the "lucky" or fortunate breaks came from strategic thinking and planning. For the other start-ups in the Liberated Learners network, the details in terms of who they met and the breaks they got to build their organizations may be different, but the basic ideas and strategies are the same.

NATHANIEL KRUGER
Princeton Learning Cooperative Teen Member

I've actually never been to public school and never had any desire to go, since the majority of public school students I talk to hate it. For most of my life I was homeschooled, first through seventh grade. I then attended a private school in Princeton for eighth grade and arrived at the Princeton Learning Cooperative for what would have been my first year

of high school but instead ended up being my first step into a whole new world of freedom and responsibilities.

I went to a Waldorf nursery school for three years. I somewhat enjoyed my time there, but when my family started homeschooling my sister, they started homeschooling me as well. My mother remembers that when she first told me I would be homeschooled, we were in the car on the way to the nursery school, and I pointed at the school and said, "Good, I don't have to go to *that* school anymore!" So at the ripe age of five, I was out of the school system.

My first couple of years of homeschooling breezed by in art classes, reading, writing, and arithmetic and just being the young child that I was and playing with my friends. I went to a lot of local homeschool groups, where I met new people and had new experiences. However, the older I got, the more academic work I had. I was still interacting with the homeschooling community, but by seventh grade most of my homeschooling friends were in school and I spent a lot of time at home. I started losing my drive and commitment to academic work. The next year, my mother was going to start working, so it was time to dive into school—something I was dreading.

I started by going to summer school at the private school I would attend that year. I remember walking into the classroom and just being completely dazed. It was such a surreal experience sitting down in a desk surrounded by a bunch of other teens. I slowly adjusted to the classroom experience and started my eighth grade year. I caught on very quickly, and my first report card came back with all As. According to the school's standards I was doing very well, but I was completely obsessed over my grades, stressed out, and not enjoying the academic work. It would often ruin my entire week if I didn't get a 100 percent on a test or project. It was just study for the test, study for the test, take the test, and study for the next test. My whole learning experience had devolved into getting that perfect score; I didn't care about any other aspect of my education. So yes, school worked for me, according to the standards set by school, but there I was, not even in high school yet and losing my mind.

The next summer, I attended the summer school program, but my parents and I were searching for an alternative. That's when they thought of the Princeton Learning Cooperative. My sister had attended PLC for parts of her sophomore and junior years, and it had been a good experience for her. I visited PLC a couple of times, and the freedom completely blew my mind, as did the friendliness of the members there. I joined PLC in 2013 for what would have been my freshman year, and I took back my life. I took it back from the grades, the stress, and the social expectations. I created, with the help of an awesome community, a whole new learning experience, a learning experience that I controlled rather than one that controlled me.

As soon as I joined PLC, I started exploring different subjects, pursuing my passions and finding new ones, and just enjoying my time. A big thing for me was being able to go outside. In school I was trapped inside, and then I had homework when I got home. I didn't really realize how much I missed the outdoors until I had the freedom to experience it in its entirety once more. As I started to regain my love of learning, I started to enjoy activities I had not found fun in the slightest in school. My attitude toward academic work completely changed, especially for one particular subject—poetry. I specifically remember in school when we had assignments relating to poetry in any way, this feeling of loathing would rise up in me. Here at PLC, when I joined a writing work-shop, we were just sharing poems, and I tried writing them, just for fun. All of a sudden instead of it being some activity that was bothersome, it became a way to express myself. Without anyone forcing me to write, I started to actually appreciate the beauty in poems.

With this freedom I was able to explore my passions of fit-ness and architecture, which helped to give me an understand-ing of what I would want to pursue in the future. It has helped me figure out what my interests are now, instead of getting to college and having no idea what I want to do or graduating with a degree in something I do not want. PLC has also helped boost my confidence and gain leadership skills. I remember when I first arrived at PLC. I would barely say anything at our group meetings. I have now led many of these same meetings. PLC has helped not only leadership in the community but also leadership in myself. I'm taking charge of *my* education and *my* future. No longer are teachers telling me what to do and when to do it by. I am responsible for how I learn and live at a whole new level. And this also helps prepare me for my future in a way that school did not. Being able to communicate with the volunteers who help me, being able to organize a community—these are valuable life skills.

Also, social life at PLC is different than being in school or being homeschooled. When I was homeschooled, it was very likely that I would be home for a couple of days and not see anyone besides my family, whereas when I was in school for five days a week I was surrounded by people and my every move was watched. I felt very judged in school. At PLC it's almost the perfect mix. I'm not isolated; at any given moment I guarantee the common room will be abuzz with friendly chatter. But I feel a lot more accepted than I was in school, and if I need time to myself, people respect that and aren't always gossiping about it.

The Princeton Learning Cooperative and its whole psychology of trust and respect have helped me grow in so many ways. I am very grateful for the community of support that PLC gives me, as well as the support of my family and friends. Instead of my main goal being to pass a test or get a good grade, it is now to pursue my dreams and passions and appreciate the freedom of choice that makes us human.

6

The inspiration for what would become Liberated Learners came from one of the North Star replication conferences in 2012. We were at the end of a three-day conference with folks from all over the country who came to learn more about the North Star model and how they could start their own program in their communities. North Star had been holding these annually since 2007, and up until this point, they had been doing all this replication work just as part of their normal operations. The programs that started, like Princeton Learning Cooperative and Compass in Ottawa, were independent organizations with obviously close ties to North Star, but there was no formal organizational relationship between the centers.

Our feeling is that self-directed learning and the North Star model are not necessarily for everyone but that it should be an option in every community in the country. Any teen who is miserable in school should have the option to leave and have the support to create the kind of life he or she wants. And it seems obvious to us that in every community there are a handful of teens who don't like school and there are a couple of teachers or other interested adults who don't like school as well. It was simply a matter of spreading the vision and helping them find each other and start a program.

We thought that to make this vision of a North Star model center in every community a reality, we would need to create an organization that was specifically focused on finding people capable of starting and running centers, consulting with them, and supporting them. We also needed to find ways for these centers to network and support each other. North Star itself would not have the attention and time to do the massive amount of work necessary to spread the vision while also continuing to run its own learning center.

The result of this thinking was Liberated Learners.

Liberated Learners was started more as an idea and a hope than a fully formed organization. So we are still evolving in response to the needs of our member centers and the time, energy, and resources that the organization has. There are a couple of crucial ways LL supports adults in learning about, creating, and sustaining North Star model centers in their communities.

For people who are just learning about the North Star model and want to investigate what it is all about, we offer a free conversation with someone from LL and an introductory webinar that goes over the basic philosophy and the educational and business model.

If people feel that this is the path they want to go down personally and professionally, LL offers support and resources to help flesh out their ideas and start the formal planning for what they want to create. The central support we offer our members in the start-up phase is mentoring by experienced founders or staff members at existing LL centers. It is hard to overstate the value of this mentoring. It can cut years off the start-up timeline and prevent a multitude of common mistakes and missteps. This step typically involves phone calls and e-mails with the LL team over the course of six months.

Part of this initial mentoring phase helps the start-ups work through a planning document, similar to a business plan, that guides the team through a number of crucial decisions about their project; such as: where it will be located, what ages of kids will they work with, how many days will it be open, what they will charge, what kind of space they will use, what will be their organization's brand identity, who will be on the team and what will their roles be, what salaries they are aiming for, how they will get the word out about what they are doing, etc.

One of the crucial things that we help with initially is developing the language to be able to speak effectively about self-directed learning. We essentially tell parents the exact opposite of everything they have ever heard about learning and raising competent kids (leave school; you don't need school to be successful). Staff members at centers need to be able to come across as credible and reliable people, as well as make this crazy thing we are asking parents to do not seem so crazy and in fact seem eminently reasonable. This is not an easy thing to do at first, and it takes years of talking with parents and teens to be able to do it fluently.

Along these same lines, Liberated Learners members are able to use all of the website language and marketing materials each center has developed for their own centers. This can cut months of work off the start-up time-line, and people can start with a fully fleshed-out website and handouts that have worked for other centers in attracting and signing up members. This also includes the forms and materials we use when families sign up, including emergency contact forms, applications, internal documents for tracking criti-cal financial numbers, and documents on how to best organize the work of the center.

Down the road, Liberated Learners hopes to have opportunities for our members to jointly hire various professional services like grant writers, mar-keting people, website developers, etc., at a low cost. For example, it doesn't make much sense for Princeton Learning Cooperative to hire a full-time grant writer. It is very unlikely that a funder would want to give large sums of money to such a small organization, but if Liberated Learners was writing the grant for an entire network of centers, gifting larger amounts of money becomes much more likely. It makes more sense for Liberated Learners to hire the grant writer as opposed to individual centers. One effort we have recently under-taken in this area is to start collecting uniform data from all of our centers on the outcomes of our teen members so that we can demonstrate to funders that this approach is working and is worthy of financial support.

Liberated Learners also runs an apprenticeship program. One of the main roadblocks to having a center in every community in the country is a lack of staff that is trained and able to work in these places. It is not really possible to just take people out of teacher training school and slot them into a staff posi-tion. The training and mindset are different. We started the apprenticeship program for people who want to either work in or eventually open up their own centers. The apprentices work for a year full-time at a center and do all the things a staff member does. They also get to see the administrative aspects of opening and running a center. The first apprentice Liberated Learners had was Justin Lanier. He spent a year at Princeton Learning Cooperative, but he was more like a staff member in the types and amount of work he did. The following year we hired him as a full-time staff member when a position opened up. This is the kind of pipeline we are hoping to create, ideally as a replacement for four years of college-based education in teacher training, as well as for people who perhaps have no background in education and are just interested in working with young people and sharing their talents.

We also host a yearly conference for Liberated Learners members. This is an invaluable experience for all of us. We come together to share what we have learned about effective ways to run our centers, discuss challenges, prioritize the work of our larger network, and celebrate our successes. Not many people do this kind of work, so gathering everyone together can give a real sense of camaraderie and purpose that might be hard to feel in each isolated center.

Liberated Learners also works to promote ourselves and our member centers as part of a growing and important movement in education. Belonging to this organization gives our centers more credibility than if we were all just small, isolated communities scattered around North America. When families ask how long we have been open or how we know this path can work for their children, we have the history and experience of all of the centers to point to and not just our small community. Belonging to a movement and feeling like you are part of creating something special is an amazing feeling, and Liberated Learners centers can share in this awesome experience. We do a number of things to promote Liberated Learners as a brand: we have a blog that contains writings from all of our member centers, we attend alternative education conferences, and we reach out to reporters and the media (we were recently mentioned in Ken Robinson's book, *Creative Schools*), among other initiatives.

As the movement toward self-directed learning grows, we think Liberated Learners will be at the forefront, inspiring others to start their own centers and supporting them in this crucial work.

SARA WEBBER

Princeton Learning Cooperative Teen Member

My experience with public education was not a pleasant one. I enjoyed school up until middle school, when I started to feel like every day was the same. I struggled with anxiety and depression throughout my high school years, which made it difficult to attend school each day. In my freshman year, I stopped going to my classes as soon as a week into the school year. At first it was just a few classes that stressed me out. Then I ended up just attending English and lunch. By November, I was too petrified to enter the building sometimes. I spent about a month in a therapy program six hours a day and slowly transitioned back into school, doing home instruction to make up for the classes that I missed. I had to get an IEP so that I could get accommodations to pass my freshman year. In my sophomore year, I realized that I wasn't learning anything. We were just focusing on me trying to stay present in class. By the end of the day, I was too emotionally exhausted to do homework, and my ADHD didn't help with that either.

I felt like I was a square cookie trying to be smooshed into a triangular cookie cutter. Everyone is different, so why teach everyone the same way? Before my junior year, I goaded my parents into looking at some alternative schools. We visited the Jersey Shore Free School, a Sudbury school in Little Silver, and South Mountain Co-op, a democratic school in Maplewood, New Jersey. My parents were just very skeptical of them because of the lack of a high school diploma. Now, I know that I don't need a high school diploma to be successful, but I didn't know that at the time. I knew that I needed an alternative path, but my parents were hesitant at the time, and they thought I would be able to push through at public school until graduation.

I pushed through my junior year until winter break. By then, I was having breakdowns almost daily and my grades were not reflecting my learning abilities. I was enrolled in a therapeutic program that my school had started that year, and no one seemed to understand that I didn't need therapy; I needed change. It was then that my mom found PLC. We found it just in time. I visited PLC on a Tuesday and the next Monday was my first day. I knew instantly that PLC was right for me. A small community of caring people, no pressure to hand in assignments, and an overall love of learning from everyone.

Since joining PLC, I've taken full advantage of the countless resources and opportunities. I became an active member of many classes and have taken leadership roles in the PLC community. I led a trip to visit evolutionary biologists Rosemary and Peter Grant, who are professors at Princeton University and have done incredible studies on Darwin's finches in the Galapagos over a span of forty years. Another PLC student and I started a recycling center in hopes of reducing PLC's waste, and it has gone incredibly. I taught multiple classes, including a six-week "short course" on gender and sexuality and a sign language class that I will be continuing in the 2015–2016 year.

PLC has helped me find out what my passions are as well. When I was in public school, I had interests, but I was so focused on schoolwork and such that I had no time to pursue my own academic interests. I've taken classes at Union County College in my time that I'm not at PLC, and I am going on a trip to Ecuador that focuses on sustainable development. Next year, I will be applying to colleges that I would never have gotten into with a GPA that didn't reflect my learning abilities at all. Thanks to PLC, I have an incredible future that is worth looking forward to and many adventures lying ahead.

Update: Sara was accepted to Hampshire College in Massachusetts early decision with a scholarship for emerging scientists.

7

Why We Started a Self-Directed Learning Center Instead of a School

There are definite perks to being a tenured teacher in a traditional public school: good wages with a built-in raise system, good health care benefits, a predictable schedule, limited hours, summer breaks, a good pension system, and essentially a job for life with very little possibility of ever being let go. These were the things everyone told me I was crazy to throw away when I quit to start PLC.

Even as I type this, I'm thinking, *Wow, that sounds pretty good.* But for me, it was not enough, and not enough of the right kind of stuff. Even with all those benefits and the security, I showed up at school every day pretty unhappy, many days miserable. In contrast, I can only think of a handful of days in the past five years of working at PLC that I wished I were somewhere else. I come home happy. People ask me how my day was, and I respond with an enthusiastic, "Great!" and I mean it. I truly enjoy how I spend my time. So, what is it about working in a self-directed learning center that is different?

1. You have freedom to teach and focus on the things you love and feel are important.

As a staff member at a self-directed learning center, you have the chance to lead classes, workshops, or one-on-one sessions on a huge variety of topics based on what you are interested in and what the teen members want.

Want to lead a class on Prohibition-era organized crime? Go for it. Want to lead a class on the ethics of eating animals? Why not? Interested in building robots and learning how to program them to pick up and recycle empty soda cans? Do it!

If you have an idea or the kids suggest something and people are interested, put it on the calendar. It's that simple.

As a staff member, I don't actually lead a lot of classes each year. My main focus is mentoring ten or eleven teens, administrative work, and leading about four classes a week. These classes tend to be small, maybe three to ten kids each. There is no grading to do. If you choose to assign optional work or the kids request it, you can offer feedback, but there are no marathon late-night paper-grading sessions. There is also no pre-determined curriculum to follow. It is truly what makes sense for your interests and the interests of the kids you have in the class.

Just to give you a flavor, here are the classes I'll be leading this upcoming year:

- Current Events—a discussion class of what is going on in the news.
- American History—what I used to teach in school.
- Evolution—an introduction to evolutionary theory. I have no formal biological training, but I have read deeply on the subject and it's a blast, so I do it. We go fossil hunting, set up trips to meet world-famous professors at Princeton, etc.
- Be More Awesomer—this is a new class I teach this year that will be about being your best self and the philosophy and tactics around that. It will also be a group in which members support each other in achieving what they want in life.

Why these classes? Because it is what I am interested in at the moment; I have some background knowledge; teens will respond to them; and some of them fit nicely into what our members have planned for their studies as they look to apply to college. Other classes I have led at various times include Basic Math, Writing for Life, the Holocaust, US Government, AP United States History, World History, The Art of Self-Directed Learning, and *Ancient Aliens* Is B.S.

Again, my main focus as a staff member is not leading classes, but the teaching I do is very rewarding because it fits my interests, the teens are there because they want to be, the administrative tasks are minimal, and since there is no curriculum to follow or tests to prepare for, the material can be alive. Plus, generally it's just fun to do.

2. Self-directed learning centers are much easier to start.
One of the great advantages of starting a self-directed learning center over a traditional private school or public charter school is that the regulatory hurdles, red tape, and financial model are much simpler. But they're still not easy.

You do not need anyone's approval to start a self-directed learning center. There are no applications to local government agencies or school boards. State bureaucracies don't regulate you. Any kind of dealings with the state fall on the families you work with as they become homeschoolers. The regulations are manageable, and you can support your families in meeting them. You will have to deal with local authorities in the sense that you will need occupancy permits for your space and some other minor things, but they will treat you as any other small business start-up in your town. There are no additional educational regulations that you must follow. Contrast this to the typical charter school application process and you'll get an idea of how much simpler the self-directed learning center process is.

The financial model is also much simpler. Again, not easy but simpler. There are very few overhead costs to start a self-directed learning center. Princeton Learning Cooperative started with $4,000 in loans from our four founders and bootstrapped the rest through low payment (or nonpayment) of salaries in the start-up phase. You don't have to follow the same formula and could raise money to pay yourself a decent salary during the start-up phase, but it is possible to start with very little money. Salaries will make up the vast majority of the money you will pay out. The other major expenses are just rent and insurance. You will not be spending thousands of dollars to buy textbooks or pay administrative staff or purchase twenty iPads or any other miscellaneous costs associated with schools. You'll likely be dealing with revenues under $500,000, and this can be managed and tracked by someone without specialized bookkeeping knowledge.

While the finances are simple—not much more complicated than your household budget—getting the numbers to work is not easy and takes a lot of hard work, just like in any other small business start-up. Getting the word out, bringing in paying members, and running a successful center is incredibly challenging, but it's no more challenging than starting a bakery or a flower shop or any other kind of new venture.

3. You will feel better and be part of something amazing.

For me, working in a self-directed learning center just meant feeling inspired and happy most days instead of frustrated, tired, unappreciated, and generally not liking my life. There are still days that are hard or routine or frustrating. Most of these days involve helping young people work through issues they might have with one another or working with families that might be in one kind of turmoil or another, but I know those occasional tough days are in service to a much larger goal that I find deeply satisfying.

It's pretty amazing to feel that you are playing a part in a movement that you think will be revolutionary and will have a big and lasting impact not only on the lives of the members you work with but also on the larger culture of education in the United States and beyond.

One of the things we talk to our members about when they join is that, unlike at the schools they came from where they may have been one of thousands of kids and felt very much like a cog in a machine, at PLC they are one of about thirty members. They have a much bigger say and responsibility in making the community the way they want it to be. If they don't like something or want to try something new, they don't have to wade through endless bureaucracies and levels of approval. The people they need to talk to can all fit in one room and have a discussion about it. This is very empowering, and realizing that they can be the captains of their own ships can be transformational for a lot of young people.

In the same way, feeling that you have ownership of the organization as a staff member can be an amazing feeling. No more sitting through pointless "professional development" workshops. No more getting crappy schedules because you are the low person on the seniority list. You get to decide when spring break is and when the year should be over. No more filling out pointless paperwork or lesson plans. You can decide for yourself what personal and professional development would be helpful for you and the organization. You can determine the nature and form of the communications to families and the kind of support and feedback that will be helpful to the teen members. Now that I've been out of the system for four years, the thought of going back in and having someone else's judgment and priorities replace my own is unthinkable.

There are also endless opportunities to grow and use skills you never thought you had. Especially in the start-up phase when you will do a bit of everything, you will tap into your whole range of talents. Just off the top of my head, I have learned or utilized the following because of my role and involvement with PLC: public speaking, bookkeeping, marketing, nonprofit management, mentoring, business development, meditation, e-mail marketing, systems, how community colleges work, college admissions, time management and getting things done, homeschooling law and practice.

I've also learned about almost every cool or interesting thing happening in and around Princeton that has any relation to teens or interning and volunteering, how to build networks of people, how to effectively communicate with large groups of people, leadership, and (currently) how to write and publish a book. There is no end to the types of things you could bring to your work in a self-directed learning center. It's this type of personal and professional development that I thought was missing in my teaching career, which is why I called in sick for almost every teacher in-service day the last couple of years of my career and why I feel that I have grown tremendously as a person and as a professional since leaving. Being involved in PLC has transformed me as well as our member families and teens.

4. The relationships are better.
When you work in traditional schools, the oftentimes bizarre relationship you are required to have with young people doesn't seem so weird. In fact, it can feel normal and natural. It's only when you view it from the outside and compare it with the relationships you have with other people in your daily life that the nature of school relationships becomes apparent.

For example, the idea that I should be in control of when a seventeen- or eighteen-year-old human can go to the bathroom, eat, get a drink, chew gum, or wear a hat is just weird. The idea that young people need to ask my permission to take care of their most basic needs only seems normal and natural in a system that relies, at its core, on coercion of varying degrees. Taken outside the context of school, controlling young people in this way is easily seen for what it is.

Some of the most touching moments at PLC occur on new members' first days when they kindly and meekly ask me if they can go to the bathroom or if they can eat lunch and I get to be the person to let them know that they never need to ask permission to pee or eat a banana ever again.

I understand the internal logic of this level of control in schools (we can't just have people roaming the halls, it's a safety issue, how can we ever get anything done in class if people are constantly not in the room, who is going to clean up the room if people are eating there, who is going to scrape the gum off the desks, etc.), but just because the internal logic makes sense in that context doesn't mean the end result is correct, makes sense, or is desirable. In the same way that nuclear arms escalation and deterrence makes internal sense (they have them, so we have them; if they launch at us, we need to be able to launch at them) and the end result of that logic (everyone dies) is no good and makes no sense at all, the controlling nature of school makes sense but ultimately defeats the entire purpose.

Another example: Have you ever asked a kid who was reading a book in your class to put it away and get back to working on whatever the class was doing? I did many times when I was a teacher, although I stopped near the end of my career. We want kids to be readers ultimately, but the logic of control and putting our priorities above theirs gets in the way. For me, the controlling and judgmental aspects of teaching (e.g., grading, progress reports, honor roll, etc.) required by the system prevented me from relating to young people the way I wanted and the way I felt would be useful to them.

They need an adult ally, someone who is on their side, someone who can help them figure out what is important to them in life (hint: it is almost never the Compromise of 1850 or the quadratic formula), someone who can give advice and listen to their concerns in a nonjudgmental way, someone who can help connect them to people, opportunities, and resources to help them get where they want to go in life, someone who will leave them alone if they don't want help, and someone who will take no for an answer.

I wanted relationships that started with trust and respect and had no hidden agendas like getting them to learn something they might not be particularly interested to know. This type of relationship thrives at self-directed learning centers. When I was teaching, I certainly felt that I treated my students with respect and trust. Almost all the teachers I worked with in my eleven years of teaching in school did the same. It is not a case of good versus bad teachers or personalities; it is a systemic issue in compulsory schools. No matter how respectful and trusting I am as an individual, the only reason my students are sitting in my class in the first place is that our current system as a whole does not trust that families will do what is in the best interest of their children and therefore compels them to be in school.

The bottom line for me is that by working in a self-directed learning center, I don't have to do anything to young people that I feel is harmful, that I feel is at odds with my sense of what is right or wrong, or that I feel is not in their best interest. That was certainly not the case when I was a teacher.

There is a lot of subtlety and nuance in the relationships we have with teens in self-directed learning centers that I won't go into here, but the relationships always start with trust and respect rather than control or rewards and punishments. Ultimately that is the kind of relationship I want with all people, including young people, because it is so rewarding and a much better way to go through life.

LIBERATED LEARNERS MEMBER PROFILE
Maria Corse, Deep Root Center for Self-Directed Learning

When I was in seventh grade, I decided that I wanted to be a home economics teacher because I was really good at it and it was just something that I wanted to do. After my children were born and then my daughter was heading to pre-K, I said to myself, "Oh my goodness, what am I going to do with myself?" That's when I went back to school and got my degree in anthropology, planning to continue and get my master of science for teachers (the teaching credential in New York State.) I got the degree in anthropology and then applied to do an internship at the only alternative school in my area with the idea that I would still do my MST. Then the director of that school said, "Why don't you just stay here and you won't have to do your MST?" I thought that was great and agreed. So that's how I became a teacher. I do not have any formal teacher training. I never took any college classes in education. I call myself more of an intuitive teacher than a trained teacher.

I worked at that alternative school for ten years. It was a two-room schoolhouse, and I was the middle teacher, which meant that I had all the kids that were between ages eight and twelve. In 2012, we brought a group of older high school students to Puerto Rico, to the International Democratic Education Conference. That completely opened my eyes to what democratic education is and what student-centered education can be. I had always done more student-led projects over the years, but after I went to the IDEC conference I felt like, *Wow! This is what education is supposed to be like!* That was pretty eye-opening for me, and I discovered that the situation at the alternative school really wasn't "that."

So after teaching at the alternative school for ten years, I was told that my methods and ideology were too alternative for that alternative space. I knew that I wanted to create a safe, inspiring, supportive space that offered kids a chance to not only have a say in their education but to quite literally be in the driver's seat. I also knew that I did not want to open a school.

After months of researching other types of alternative education, I stumbled upon North Star (which happened to be located in the town where my son was going to college), and it was exactly what I had been searching for. I quit my job in the middle of the spring semester and attended the Liberated Learners conference in July, and because of the phenomenal support I received from Kenneth, Joel, and the other members of Liberated Learners, the Deep Root Center pilot program opened the following January.

Running a center is so completely different from working in a school. I'm doing things that I never thought I would ever do. Even though we only have a few members so far, I'm feeling so confident in putting this idea out to anybody I talk to. That's pretty life changing, to discover that you can talk about something completely passionately with no reservations, saying, "This will help you, and I can help you make your life different or make your life better." It's empowering for me, and it's also empowering for the people I'm talking to. This one kid who has just signed on, his mother had been hassled by the local school district about attendance and homework and she was at wit's end. I was able to say, "Look, this is what we're going to do. We're going to get them off your back." I could just feel and hear the relief from her, and that's pretty amazing to be able to do that for people.

Just walking down the street with a Deep Root Center shirt on and having people come up to me and ask me about it feels amazing. Normally, I'm not that kind of person. Being passionate about something and then being able to express that to the community is very new for me. It has come out in other ways, too, like blogging, which is one powerful way to get the message out. I have a lot of time to write, and my writing skills have skyrocketed.

8

Operational Considerations

One of the challenging parts of starting your own self-directed learning center is that many teachers do not have a lot of business background or experience running an organization. That was certainly true in my case. I started essentially at zero knowledge of the legal, financial, marketing, and practical necessities of creating PLC when I attended that first replication conference at North Star in 2007. While challenging, the process of learning as much as I could about these topics as we were building and running PLC was among the most satisfying experiences I have had. And in true self-directed learning style, all of the knowledge I have gained in these areas has come from experience, conversations with people I've sought out, books, fortunate coincidences, mentors, and podcasts.

What follows in this chapter is not a comprehensive and complete statement of every little detail you will need to know to start a center, but it will be enough to familiarize you with the basic terminology, concepts, and resources that will get you going on your own journey.

THE MOST IMPORTANT IDEAS YOU'LL LEARN FROM THIS SECTION

- Build a team.
- Create something that people want to tell their friends about.
- Focus on helping teens leave school, not on collecting existing homeschoolers.
- Charge enough to make it work financially.

LEGAL STRUCTURE AND PROCESS

Forms, forms, and more forms. Filling out forms is one of the big job requirements to get started. In this section, I'll talk about a couple of the major forms that you will be filling out as you create your center and what they are for.

First, I will describe the process of starting a nonprofit center.

I can imagine for-profit ways of running a self-directed learning center, in which case you would create a limited liability company (LLC), an S corp, a sole proprietorship, or some other legal structure. But there are a couple of reasons why all Liberated Learners centers are nonprofits. First, as a nonprofit, people's donations can be written off their taxes, which encourages financial support. Also, the model relies very heavily on volunteers and federal work-study college students. In the case of work-study students, it's not required that you be a nonprofit, but the work has to be in the public interest, which is a no-brainer if you are a nonprofit. Also, I would imagine very few people would be willing to volunteer their time if the center was operating for profit. They would probably want to be paid something, which complicates the financial model.

The first step in the process of forming a nonprofit is to identify who is going to be involved in the organization. By law you will need to form a board of directors (in some states called trustees) in order to file incorporation papers in your state. Unlike a private company, a board of directors in a nonprofit is technically the "owning" entity and is responsible for the financial and legal health of the organization, as well as making sure the organization carries out its mission.

The ideal team for your board of directors includes people who have skills and knowledge that can support your organization. For example, it is good to have a lawyer on the board, an accountant, someone with a marketing background, a designer, someone who is good at raising money, and some educators. This is the ideal arrangement. But typically what happens at the start up of small nonprofits is you will just get some friends to be on the board or, really, anyone willing to show up for the meetings. If you start identifying and recruiting board members who have the kinds of skills you will eventually want from the very beginning, you'll be able to have a high-performing board sooner.

You will also want to make sure the role of the board is clearly defined. Board members are rightfully involved in oversight and guidance but not the day-to-day management of the center. When the organization is small, sometimes board members play a more important role in the day-to-day activities simply to support the staff, but ultimately it is the staff's responsibility to carry out the mission of the organization through their work with young people.

There are a lot of ways to organize a board, and these will be spelled out in a document called the bylaws. Bylaws are required to file incorporation papers. It is basically a list of rules about how the organization will work, including how often the board will meet, what the roles of officers will be, what happens if board members don't attend meetings, voting rules, etc. Examples of boilerplate bylaws are available online, and you can adapt them to the wishes of the board.

Once you have your board in place, have chosen a name, and have some draft bylaws drawn up, you can submit incorporation papers to your state as a nonprofit corporation. This essentially creates a new entity that can carry out legal functions in its name as opposed to your personal name. This means the new organization can open a checking account, get a credit card, and purchase insurance. The incorporation process is typically pretty quick and does not require a lawyer to complete. Members of Liberated Learners have access to the state incorporation documents that our member centers have filed.

Once you get the incorporation papers back from the state, you can now file with the federal Internal Revenue Service for what is called an employer identification number (EIN). This is basically like a social security number for your organization. It enables the IRS and other government agencies to identify you. The process to obtain an EIN is very simple and can be done online or over the phone very quickly.

Before you start to operate and work with young people, another thing you want to do is to purchase insurance. Princeton Learning Cooperative carries a couple of different types of insurance, and we work with an insurance broker to find the right kind of insurance for the best price. The first kind of insurance we carry is called directors and officers liability insurance (D&O). This basically protects your board of directors from being personally responsible if the organization is sued for any reason. Many experienced board members might not join your board unless you have this, so you will want to get it. We also carry general liability insurance, which is for slips and falls or any other potential issues that might come up in connection to the physical building you use or your operations. The last type of insurance we carry is professional liability insurance, which covers us if someone sues us for malpractice. For example, someone could say that because of our actions and incompetence, their child did not get into college. Professional liability insurance would cover us against any claim like that. Your state will also likely require you to carry workers' compensation insurance. There are a lot of other kinds of insurance, but those are the basics and what we carry at PLC.

At this point if you have a board, an EIN number, insurance and have identified who will be on staff, you could open your doors and start working with families. Many of our centers open at this point even though they are not officially recognized as nonprofits by the federal government.

The last step in the process of getting nonprofit designation is to file form 1023 with the IRS to be recognized as a tax-exempt organization (the more accurate term for a nonprofit). Once this is completed and approved, you will be recognized as a 501c3 organization by the federal government, and you will not need to pay taxes on the money you bring in. Donors will also be able to make contributions that are tax-deductible.

Form 1023 is longer and more complicated than the incorporation documents for the state, but Liberated Learners members have access to the 1023s we have filed that have been approved, which should eliminate the need to hire a lawyer. There is a fee of around $1,000 to file the application, and the IRS turnaround time can be significant, which is why many organizations start operating before they receive their official designation.

As a 501c3 organization, you will be required to file a 990 tax form each year, which is like a tax return for tax-exempt organizations. If you make under a certain amount of revenue, there is a very simple and easy form you can submit, but if you have higher revenue, you must file the longer version. We typically have an accountant prepare this for us.

Thinking of yourself as a tax-exempt organization instead of a nonprofit is important in the financial and business planning you will be doing. When many people think nonprofit, they think they will not be bringing in enough money to sustain their operations and will have to depend on donations or grants to keep the doors open. Others think they will always be working on a shoestring budget and will be unable to pay themselves a living wage. These are both misconceptions that are vitally important to steer clear of if you hope to be open more than two years.

Tax-exempt means just that: you don't have to pay taxes on the revenue you generate. It does not mean you have to operate in poverty or that you can't take in more money than you spend. The only thing that really changes about how you run your business is that whatever money is left over after expenses cannot be distributed to shareholders or others as profit; the money must remain in the organization and be used for your tax-exempt purposes, which in this case is education.

START-UP FUNDS AND BUDGETS

The nice thing about the North Star model is that the finances are very simple to understand. However, making the budget work, like in any organization, is challenging. There are really only three main expenses in the model, the biggest being salary for staff followed by rent and then insurance. There are very few expenses for supplies or other miscellaneous costs. (See PLC's budgets for the first two years in the appendix.)

Start-up funding can be handled in a couple of ways. Almost all of the Liberated Learners centers have started by bootstrapping, which means you do not start with a huge pile of money but fund the start-up mostly through nonpayment of salary. PLC started with $4,000 in loans, $1,000 from each of the four founding board members, and then we brought in money through tuition fees to pay salary and insurance and rent that first year. At PLC, we had what was called the "year of pain" for new staff members, which basically meant a year in which you did not make a lot of money. The first year we opened, we paid about $15,000 in compensation to our single staff member. The following year when I came on staff, the original staff member made $40,000 and I made $16,000 or so - my year of pain. When our next staff member came on, she had a year of pain. If you were to total up the amount of pay cuts the entire staff took over the three to four years of our start-up, it is substantial—probably in the $300,000 range. This is how we funded the start-up.

While bootstrapping may sound impossible and seem like a recipe for disaster, there are some distinct advantages to starting that way. The first is that you are not spending a lot of time and effort trying to secure funding either through donations or loans. It helps you stay focused on what will ultimately be the source of continued success: finding, recruiting, and doing good work with families. Another advantage to bootstrapping is the "hustle" factor. If you borrow money to pay yourself a salary during the start-up, you could be lulled into a false sense of security or have a lack of urgency around doing the work that needs to be done to build the organization and make it sustainable. When you are staring at a big fat zero for your paycheck, you need to bring in another paying member, so you tend to be more motivated to make that next call or plan that next event.

You can imagine other ways of raising the money to get started. If you want to cover all expenses and pay the two founding staff members a living salary for the first two years, you will likely need to raise somewhere between $300,000 and $350,000 dollars. You could do this by using some of your personal savings, getting donations, applying for grants, or taking out a small business loan from a bank (though this is unlikely.) Recently, one of our Liberated Learner centers raised a significant amount of money to open a center in an economically depressed area, but it took a tremendous amount of work and effort to pull it off successfully. You can also think of a situation in which other revenue--generating activities support the organization, such as owning and renting out a building and using the rent money to fund operations.

PLC has avoided going into debt to finance our start-up, and we don't rely on donations or grants to fund our basic operations. We feel it brings in an element of risk and weakness to the organization. If we rely on that big donor or grant each year to meet our budget and then the person decides not to give or the granting agency decides to change their priorities, we would be in serious trouble and might have to close like so many other well-intentioned organizations who rely on grants to survive. We weren't comfortable having that hanging over our heads every year or with taking time away from working with our families to write grants and fundraise. Our model has been to be sustainable from the money we bring in from fees and to use grants and donations to provide reserves or to fund special projects like opening new centers.

In comparison to what public schools pay teachers in our area, we are well below average, but we do very well compared to other alternative and private schools. We don't offer a health-care package at PLC, but other Liberated Learners centers do. PLC staff either get insurance through a spouse or buy it privately and use their salary to pay the premium. We do have a retirement plan set up (a SIMPLE IRA) that staff can divert some of their salary into. Staff are also part of the Social Security system.

PRICING

Another important consideration is what your fees are going to be. When we started PLC, we had no experience or frame of reference for how much we should charge, so we just pulled a number out of a hat: $8,000 a year for the pilot program year and then we bumped it to $12,000 a year when I came on staff during our second year. We didn't really have any plan or analysis, but luckily it turned out that $12,000 a year was the magic number for us and allowed us to have the income necessary to really make it work.

We recommend that Liberated Learners start-ups work backward when pricing. Figure out how much it is going to cost to run the center, including sustainable salaries for staff and funds to build reserves for lean times. All of the Liberated Learners centers work with families who can't afford the full fees, and we offer significant fee reductions in some cases to make sure the centers are economically diverse. You can count on at least 33 percent reductions in fees. In PLC's case, now we are charging $12,600 per year (we increase fees by $200 per year automatically to keep up with increases in insurance and rent) and take in on average about $8,300 per member. Our model is based on having thirty or thirty-one members each year.

So add up the likely net income from your number of members and compare it against what you need to run the center. You may need to push the fees a bit higher to make the numbers work, or perhaps you can adjust them down if possible.

We recommend keeping the fees higher and maintaining a clear and consistent message that says, "We will work with you on the cost if you need a fee reduction. If you feel this is the right place for your son or daughter, we will make the finances work." You want the fees to be high enough so that even with fee reductions you are earning enough from fees and fundraising to keep the place going.

From a marketing perspective, you also don't want to appear to be a cheap alternative. Pricing sends signals about quality. You provide a valuable service that will be absolutely life changing for some families. It is absolutely worth it, and it is not being provided by anyone else nearby. Your pricing should reflect that.

TARGET MARKET

There is a definite target market for your organization and also one common pitfall in building a membership for the center.

Rather than long-time homeschoolers, the target market you should always keep in mind is children in school who will leave and are probably considering homeschooling for the first time. It can be very tempting to try to attract existing homeschoolers as your member base, but it is a problem in disguise. While it seems like an easy and good thing to do, and in many ways it is, you should never lose focus of the fact that you are primarily looking to help kids leave the system. There are a couple of reasons for this.

First, it seems like existing homeschoolers are a great fit. They are already out of school, they get the whole idea of homeschooling, and they may have already gone through the detox period of becoming self-directed learners. All of these things are true. Existing homeschoolers have been some of the best members we've had at PLC, and North Star has had the same experience. But there is a potential problem with having a high number of existing homeschoolers as your members. Homeschooling families have often already built a life for themselves and don't look to you for the level of support that people leaving school need. Therefore, they most often want to be part-time members, attending a day or two a week. The part-time nature of their membership can make it hard to build community. Second, they typically will not be interested in paying you for a full-time membership, which will make finances a challenge if you primarily work with existing homeschoolers. Finally, many times home-schoolers will look at PLC for specific content areas that they do not cover in the their homeschooling. While PLC has a lot of great classes and tutors, being a content provider is not what we do best; neither is it our main focus.

For example, if we have an existing homeschooler who signs up for one day a week, really wants to learn Japanese, and pays us for that day, that seems great. But volunteers often need to stop volunteering abruptly for various reasons—health issues, a new job, a change in schedule, etc. We often can't find a replacement volunteer, so we now have a member who pays us for something we don't offer and is not happy about that situation because he or she isn't getting what he or she paid for. We rely almost entirely on word of mouth advertising to bring in new members, so we don't want dissatisfied or even satisfied but unenthusiastic members walking around in the community. We want people who shout our praises from the mountaintop and usually those are people who left an unsatisfying school experience and are now having a great experience at PLC.

SPACE AND LOCATION

The selection of the geographical area in which to start your center and also the physical space you will use are critical. First, you want to be in an area that has the population and resources to support your center.

Liberated Learners helps our start-ups analyze the population demographics of a proposed start-up area in terms of the number of teens in a twenty-mile radius, median family income, and poverty indicators. We also look at what kinds of alternative lifestyle organizations are already operating in the area, such as yoga studios, health food stores, and farmers markets. People who like these kinds of things are typically interested in what we are doing.

There are Liberated Learners members in more rural areas or areas with higher levels of poverty. In these cases, the funding mix will be more skewed toward donations and grants because families will have less money to contribute in fees. In the case of rural areas, recruiting new members to achieve a critical mass where the program feels vibrant is difficult.

Choosing a space to house the program is also an important consideration. Starting out, a number of Liberated Learners centers have successfully used shared spaces such as a church basement or a cultural center in town that does programming in the evening but is available during the day. This is good because the rent is typically cheaper and the facility usually includes electric, Internet, and cleaning in the rent. Whatever space you choose, you want it to be safe, warm, and inviting. You also want it to communicate the values of the organization to your member families and to visitors.

Finding a space in a part of town where parents feel comfortable with their kids walking down the street to the store unaccompanied is important, too. We have found that the best physical arrangement for what we do is one big room that everyone can fit in to use for meetings and as a common room to hang out in and then a series of smaller rooms around it that can be used for mentoring meetings, classes, or tutoring. The rooms don't have to be big because classes typically range from two to five people and there is a lot of one-on-one tutoring.

Where your center is situated in relation to a town center, public transit lines, shopping centers, local colleges, or open space is important as well. A very removed and isolated space is not ideal. Since the children (in PLC's case teens) are free to come and go from the center throughout the day, it is good to be within walking distance of someplace to go. Kids really enjoy having the freedom and responsibility to walk down to the shopping center to get lunch with their friends or go walking through the woods when they want to. For North Star it is critical to be located on the bus line. They have a number of work-study college students who come and tutor, and many of them arrive by bus. PLC is not near a bus line, but it is not critical for us because we rely more on community volunteers who have their own transportation and less on college students who do not.

STAFFING

There is no one right way to staff your center. Inside the Liberated Learners network, centers have tried a couple of variations, but I will mostly talk about the model we have developed at Princeton Learning Cooperative.

We decided to go with a full-time staff and volunteer model. We limit our community of teens to about thirty or thirty-one each year, and we have three full-time paid staff and a full-time apprentice who is paid a small stipend. We don't hire part-time staff, but some of the other Liberated Learners centers have and they have done well using that model. The reason we only do full-time staff is because we want to keep salaries as high as possible. If we hired part-timers to come one or two days a week, that would bleed some of the salary from our core staff. The upside of having part-time staff is that you can get amazing people to come do really cool stuff with members on a consistent basis and not have some of the unpredictability that comes with finding and utilizing volunteers. Depending on how you price your memberships and the budget you draw up, you could include space for part-time staff.

We also work with what we call our extended staff. This is a group of about thirty or so community members, parents, or college students who are eligible for federal work study who lead classes or tutor members on a weekly basis. They are usually scheduled for an hour one day a week, but some of our extended staff spend more time at PLC. We could not run without the support and amazing talents of this group of people. They provide classes and tutoring on a wide range of topics and interests that the core staff would never be able to do. Our board has decided that we should run background checks on all the volunteers we work with in New Jersey, and the state of Pennsylvania requires anyone working with youths to have a background check. The recruiting, scheduling, and management of our extended staff is almost a full-time job in itself.

The core staff's job is not mainly to lead classes, although we all lead around four classes each week. The bulk of our time is devoted to one-on-one mentoring sessions with our teens. We each have ten or eleven mentees that we meet with every week individually for an hour or a half hour depending on the teen and his or her needs. These mentoring sessions can include setting up classes, discussing opportunities that members are interested in, or helping them find internships or other opportunities in the wider community. They can also include documenting what the member is learning, helping with the college admissions process, or helping to set up a career path if that is the direction in which the teen is headed.

Sometimes the mentoring is strictly business: How are classes going? Anything that could be going better? Do you want to try this new class that is starting? And sometimes teens share more personal concerns or challenges. We're not a therapeutic center and our staff has no special training, but sometimes just listening or giving advice on how to handle a situation is helpful. If we witness serious at-risk behaviors, we make sure the parents are aware. We have also referred some of our families to local therapists if it seems appropriate or if they ask us for a recommendation.

The core staff is also responsible for the administration of the program. Duties are divided up according to interest, skill, and what needs to get done. This could include bookkeeping, setting up family meetings, marketing our public events, running open houses, getting background checks for our volunteers, creating budgets, dealing with insurance and the IRS, etc.

We don't require any specialized training or credentials for our core staff. Fundamentally, above all else, the staff's role in this enterprise is to build trusting, respectful relationships with our teens, their families, and the larger community.

BRAND IDENTITY

When people think of your organization, what kinds of images and vibes do you want to give? Identity is one of the critical pieces of starting any kind of business, but it is particularly critical in this case because this education model relies so heavily on relationships with your member families. The identity you develop as an organization ideally flows through everything you do, big and small, and will have an impact on the types of families you attract.

Princeton Learning Cooperative has developed a professional identity for our organization: reliable, steady, solid, competent, and friendly. You can imagine other brand identities for self-directed learning centers: artsy and whimsical, new age, workshop or makerspace, counter cultural. There is a lot of possible variation, but it is important to have a sense of who you are as an organization because it will impact your day-to-day operations and the types of messages you communicate about your program.

For example, because PLC went for a professional identity, and because one of the key types of families we wanted to draw from were professionals, in Princeton everything we do has to reflect that. Our website, business cards, flyers, and other materials all have to be high quality and look professionally designed. Handwritten black-and-white flyers that look slapped together at the last minute will not appeal to the families we want to attract—families who have the ability to support our center financially. On the other hand, if your identity is more countercultural, handwritten DIY flyers might be exactly the thing to appeal to your ideal family.

In the same way, our daily operations have to reflect our identity. We want to appear professional, mainstream, and reliable because we ask families to pull their children out of school (which already seems scary enough) and give us a large chunk of money. If we seem flaky or unreliable, that is going to erode the trust that is so critical to making our organization work. So we return phone calls and e-mails promptly, always within twenty-four hours and usually within an hour or two depending on the nature of things. We show up on time for meetings. When we say we are going to do something or send along some information to our families, we use task management software to make sure we follow through and at the right time. We don't bash schools in our materials or in public appearances because we want to be appealing to mainstream families who might have another child in school even if one of their children comes to us.

All of these little signs of reliability go a long way in establishing trust, helping parents feel that they are making the right decision for their children, and letting them know that we are here to support them.

MARKETING AND OUTREACH

We've found that the most effective way to let people know about our centers is through word of mouth, one-on-one conversations, public events that we sponsor, and newspaper articles written about us. Paid advertising is essentially useless and should be avoided.

The number one best thing to bring in members is the positive recommendations our families make to their friends and associates. We can talk and talk about our program, but nothing beats a personal recommendation from a trusted friend or coworker who has his or her own child in the program. So the best marketing you can ever do is creating and running a good program that changes kids' lives and inspires your families to tell everyone they know about this amazing place where they send their kids.

When we first started PLC, we only had staff at our open houses and info sessions, but we realized after a few years that the best people to have at the open houses were our current members and parents. So we now work with some of our members to become PLC ambassadors and train them to participate in our public events and tell their, often amazing, stories.

We also put on a series of public events called Outside the Box. These can be movies relating to education, panel discussions on a variety of topics like college admissions or mental health, or guest speakers talking about a particular topic. These public events serve a number of interlocking goals and were pretty critical in PLC's development.

The first thing these events do is get our name circulating in the wider community. We publicize them with flyers in local coffee houses and libraries. We create EventBrite listings or Meetup.com groups and those gain some traction. We send a mass e-mail to our list, including local media, and then the announcements are listed in the print media. Sometimes, the papers will put in a little item about the event, and in the past we have had journalists then want to do a feature story on PLC as an organization. It is not every day that an organization comes along telling young people and their families that it is okay to leave school, so what we do is inherently interesting and newsworthy. A front-page article in one of the local free newspapers is what really accelerated PLC's growth in the early years.

Secondly, these events let us reach out and serve the different communities that we then rely on to get the word out. In the case of the college admissions panels, we hopefully connect with the existing homeschooling community and provide something of value for them. We have three to four admissions counselors from local colleges come and talk about their admissions policies for homeschoolers, and then the audience gets to ask questions. It's valuable for homeschoolers as well as our families who are new to homeschooling and just need to hear from the people in charge that their kid can go to college without attending high school.

For the mental health panels, we get to approach local therapists to be on the panel, meet with them, and let them know about our program. This is valuable for them because they work with young people for whom school is obviously not a fit and there are very few good alternatives that they can recommend to families. In the Princeton area, it seems like the first thing families do when their kids are not doing well in school is consult a therapist. We have received a large number of referrals from the local therapists that we have connected with through these panels. Plus, the actual event draws in some families and again gets our name out into the community.

We have a table at a number of community festivals and farmers markets in the area, too, which lets us build our e-mail list and reach families who would never hear of us in other ways. This is also one of the big ways we recruit new volunteers to work in our program. We've spoken in front of Rotary groups, a professional networking organization, and local chambers of commerce as well.

One of the other strategies that has worked very well for us and other Liberated Learners centers is simply meeting face-to-face with people in the community. The strategy is just to get in front of anyone who is willing to listen and let them know about what we are doing and to hear about their work. There are certain people in the community who seem to know every interesting person and all the new and exciting things happening, and they will be able to connect you to the people who want to know about your program. The goal is to sit down with all of them face-to-face, start to build a relationship, and let them know about what you are doing. Lighthouse in Holyoke, Massachusetts, set the Liberated Learners network standard for this approach. They had more than two hundred meetings with community members before they ever opened their doors. Just about everyone in Holyoke who needed to know they were opening knew about it, and Lighthouse was able to secure some major funding and opened with about twenty teens.

Catherine Gobron, cofounder of Lighthouse and long-time staff member at North Star, put it this way in an e-mail to the Liberated Learners Google group:

LightHouse is doing well, and the biggest reason for that, I believe, is because we've been very successful in building relationships and connections in our new community.

I don't want to get ahead of myself. To be clear, LightHouse has a ways to go before we are financially stable. We've been having a lot of success, but we are not yet, "successful." I want to be clear about that. Not at all done yet. Very much in progress.

However, we are all getting paid, and while there is a fair amount of stress and uncertainty yet, the program is also thriving, and we're having the profound effects on teens' lives that we're all familiar with. We have twenty-five students enrolled, several more at the door, and three new applicants for the fall. In addition, most students are expected to return. It seems very possible that we will reach our capacity next year. We're feeling very good about it.

I'm sharing this to get to this point: Josiah and I read and studied lots of great books and resources (in addition to being immersed in this work for many years). But the number one most useful and important thing we have done so far has been our focus on building a strong base of support and connections in our new community.

We have lots and lots of collaborations going with other nonprofits and other businesses—win-wins all over town. Nearly all of our students have come to us as recommendations from these many partners. We could not possibly do this in isolation. Both Josiah and I each have several meetings per week with existing and new connections. It's a huge part of our jobs, and I think this focus is the driver behind our tentative success. It's seldom clear what will come from these connections at first. Things unfold over time. Keep a long view.

The world is ready for what we do and actively looking for us, whether they know it or not. This model has not necessarily "arrived," but we are approaching, for sure.

As your organization matures and you have done good work for teens and their families, having them do written or filmed testimonials that you can put on your website or other outlets is key, especially if you can highlight kids who have come to you with the usual mix of concerns about schools—anxiety, homework, stress. Many times when people join, they say that the testimonials they read on our website almost perfectly described the situation they were facing with their own children and were a big reason why they gave us a call.

SYSTEMS

As you create your organization, thinking about it from a systems approach is a good idea. At PLC, we found a book called *The E-Myth Revisited* by Michael Gerber to be useful. The basic idea is that your organization needs to do certain things to fulfill its mission—serve your families—and it must do them consistently and with high quality and reliability. Instead of relying on the staff's goodwill or personal qualities, it is useful to build systems that can be managed by the staff and ensure to the best of the organization's ability that these things will happen every time.

For example, one of the goals of our organization is to make sure that potential members who visit feel welcome and included and realize that our organization is special, and that after they join we help them integrate into our community. Below is the outline of the system we have created to ensure this process happens every time:

Goal: To be welcoming and enthusiastic about this wonderful choice they are making. We start building a trusting relationship with the family, which is at the core of what we do, and we set the stage for support for both the members and the parents.

1. Initial contact from family. Try to encourage most of the discussion to be at an in-person meeting with the family or just the parents as opposed to over the phone or through e-mail.
    a. When we get an inquiry, create a new line in the prospects sheet. Right click on the top-most name and select "add row above."
    b. Copy and paste the top row into the new row.

    c. Add date. Put 1 for the total. Add the name of the family and child and age if known.

    d. Enter level:

        i. 2 = active prospect, we think they might join

        ii. 1 = want to keep on the radar, but not actively seeking membership

        iii. 0 = too young, but in the pipeline for later

    e. Put a 1 in each column that applies.

    f. When a decision to apply or not has been made, put a 1 for applied and a 0 for not applied.

2. Encourage potential member to visit for a day. (Can be combined with step 1.)

    a. When a visit is scheduled, inform teen ambassadors and ask them to spend time with potential member during his or her visit.

3. During the visit:

    a. Write a welcome note on the board so everyone knows a visitor will be in the space and can refer to it to remember his or her name.

    b. Joel waits outside for the visitor to arrive to make sure he or she can find the entrance. He also plays guitar while waiting so that when the visitors arrive, they are greeted by music, which indicates immediately without any words being said that this is a special place and not your typical school.

    c. One staff member takes the first thirty minutes or hour of the visit to explain what is going on, answer any questions, review the calendar for the day, and introduce the visitors to current members with similar interests.

    d. Each staff member spends time with the potential member throughout the day.

    e. Staff encourages members to reach out and include the visitor in activities, hanging out, classes, and lunch.

    f. At least one staff member checks in with the visitor (and parents, if possible) before they leave to get a feel for how their day went and to answer any questions, help frame what they experienced that day, etc.

g. Toward the end of the visit, staff members check in with the ambassadors to get their impressions.

h. Staff quickly meets to decide if the visitor is a good candidate.

i. Staff e-mails parents either that night or the next morning to check in about how the day went and suggest next steps. We also offer to put them in touch with current or former parents if they would like.

4. If they are interested in joining, e-mail them the application form and ask them to fill it out and send it back in via e-mail or mail. For completed applications:

a. Create a folder in the drive under Member Applications.

b. Scan all pages to a PDF file, upload to the new member folder, and e-mail the PDF to staff.

c. Make or update (be sure to search for the contact before creating a new one) a contact for the member and each parent or guardian. Add name and e-mail addresses, and add to these groups: mailing list, applicant.

d. File originals in member binder.

5. Once we decide to offer membership, we send the enrollment packet for them to fill out and set up a family meeting. For completed enrollment paperwork:

a. Scan all pages to a PDF file, upload to the new member folder (move folder from applications folder to PLC Members) and e-mail the PDF to staff.

b. Update contact information to include:

i. address

ii. phone numbers (mobile and home for each person)

iii. birthday (for member)

iv. emergency information (for member)

v. parent directory, yes or no (for parents)

vi. notes (e.g., for families where a parent has a different last name, include a note as to names of the member and the other parent)

    c. Add or remove each contact to appropriate groups.

        i. Remove from applicant and interested families.

        ii. For member, add or confirm: my contacts, mailing list, all-plc, 1members.

        iii. For parents, add or confirm: my contacts, mailing list, all-plc, parents.

    d. Add allergies and photo permission info to PLC member list under notes.

    e. Make a copy of the emergency form and file it in the green emergency forms binder.

    f. File originals in member binder.

    g. Add checks from the "Helping with PLC Outreach" form to Family Outreach spreadsheet.

6. Send a proposed invoice based on the information in their application with the enrollment packet and negotiate what the fees will be in advance of the family enrollment meeting.

7. At enrollment meeting, have as much of the staff there as possible to:

    a. go over the paperwork;

    b. brainstorm ideas;

    c. determine mentor;

    d. give out bumper magnets, yard signs, T-shirts;

    e. go over what the support notes look like and how to access them; and

    f. generally celebrate this fantastic new journey the young person is starting.

8. Mentor meets with the new member on the first day and gets him or her all set up by doing the stuff on the support notes template checklist.

9. Two days in, mentor sends an e-mail to the parents asking how things are going, sets up a time for the one-month check-in family meeting, and offers to put them in touch with an experienced PLC parent.

We are working on having systems like this for every aspect of what we do, not to lock us into a certain bureaucratic way of doing things forever but to have our current method in an external form that can be shared with new staff members for training so that everyone in the organization can be on the same page. It can be reviewed to see if it is working the way we want it to and to see where improvements can be made. It might seem like a lot of work, but you will automatically have a system for doing everything, whether you consciously create one or not. It is simply the way you will get the work done in the organization. We have chosen to be explicit about how we do things and to have goals for how well we accomplish these tasks.

PERSONAL PRODUCTIVITY AND NOT LOSING YOUR MIND

When I worked as a teacher, I definitely thought I was busy. Lots of things to grade and plan. Generally, though, I could keep all of the things that needed to be done in my head and remember them when I needed to because there wasn't a crush of details and things that required my attention. I quickly learned that this system of just remembering what I needed to do was not going to cut it when I started working at PLC.

There were simply way too many details to keep track of, and things started to fall through the cracks. I would say I was going to send an e-mail with some information to someone in a meeting and then it would get lost in the sea of other to-do items and not get done. This is a problem in our work because we try to build trust and reliability with people. Following through on these small commitments in a timely manner is one way to start building trust that we are a solid and respectable organization that can get things done for your children. If we're constantly losing things or not doing what we say we are going to do, it makes us look bad as an organization.

Out of sheer necessity, I started writing things down on a piece of paper and then crossing them off when they were done—the basic to-do list. This sufficed for a while until I started to have pages and pages of items. Some were things I was waiting on from other people, and there really wasn't a system to know when things needed to be done; they were all just lumped together on the list. So any time I was figuring out what I needed to be doing, I waded through pages of scratched-out tasks, trying to find the thing I needed to do. This was time-consuming and inefficient to say the least.

At some point, I came across the work of David Allen and his book, *Getting Things Done.* His method was a godsend and probably doubled or tripled my productivity and reliability. When I said I was going to do something and when, it always happened as long as I put it into the system he recommended. I won't go into the details of the method, but you should buy the book and start practicing it. The basic idea is that our brain is terrible at remembering what to do, so you should take everything you need to do and get it out of your head and into an external form that you can review. That way your brain is freed up to be creative and focus on the actual doing of the work. I combined his method with a free program called Evernote, and it was amazing and saved me from losing my mind.

Along with working with a partner to create your program so you don't burn out trying to do everything yourself, having a reliable system for your personal productivity is highly recommended.

We also started to implement the same idea at the team level at PLC and Bucks Learning Cooperative. We use a project management software called Asana. This allows us to know what the team is focused on, who is responsible for the work, and when it needs to be done. Again, this is a game changer in terms of keeping things organized and following through on commitments. The earlier you can build this kind of communication and organization into the culture of your staff and board, the better.

There is obviously a lot of detail and nuance to the operations of a center like PLC or other Liberated Learners centers. The most important thing to remember is to not get lost in all the details and the crunch of to-do items. The top priority at any given time is to build positive and trusting relationships with the teens and families you serve.

LIBERATED LEARNERS
MEMBER PROFILE

Alison Snieckus, Princeton Learning Cooperative

My plan in high school and early college was to be a veterinarian. Teaching was not on my radar screen, but life circumstances rerouted me to a bachelor's degree in elementary education. The seeds of my interest in the alternative side of education were sown in those early years. I have a copy of *How Children Fail* by John Holt among the college books I've kept, and I did my senior thesis on the Hidden Curriculum in schools.

I only worked as a teacher in traditional K–12 schools for three years. I left when I was twenty-five after a deeply stressful year that included a disagreement with a particularly influential family in the school who had a child in my class and what I felt was a lack of support from the administration. In an effort to find my way forward, I went back to school, where I earned a master's degree in learning cognition and development. From there, I went to work as an entry-level assistant in the stats department at Educational Testing Service; I worked on the NTE tests to start, which were then transformed into the Praxis tests currently used in the teacher certification process.

When it was time for my own kids to go to school, I surveyed all the options available and we decided to go with the local K–3 public school, but it became obvious pretty quickly that neither son was a good fit for school. The issues ranged from disorganization (in first grade the teacher complained about the constant ring of items surrounding his desk) to difficulty memorizing math facts and spelling words (the second grade teacher said if he could do well on these—which he couldn't, though we tried and tried—he could use the electricity kit, which he loved and sat unused in the corner).

As the issues piled up in those early years, undermining their self-worth and our home life, I came upon the idea to homeschool.

Looking back, I think the issue was more that I couldn't deal with the traditional school system. I was deeply frustrated because the teachers didn't accommodate my sons' strengths and weaknesses (and I couldn't seem to advocate for what was needed), and in the process the system disrespected them in many small ways. I got the brunt of my children's frustrations in the later afternoon and evening; it seemed like I was allocated the worst part of their waking hours! We were well suited to the homeschooling lifestyle and continued through high school. During this time, another mom and I started a weekly group for homeschooling teens called E-Cubed.

Through my homeschooling connections, I learned that Joel and Paul were starting Princeton Learning Cooperative based on the North Star model. I had read about North Star and had seriously considered starting a center of my own (it seemed like the obvious next step to expand our weekly group to a full-time offering), so when I saw there was going to be a program in our area, I knew I had to be involved. I started as a board member shortly after the founding of PLC and became a staff member in the second year.

Working at PLC has changed my life in so many positive ways. I enjoy supporting kids to educate themselves without traditional school and helping them see that everything they do in life can "count" as part of their education. It makes me feel really good to trust kids with their own learning and with a larger role in our community. I love that we can value each individual person and what he or she brings to the table. We get to help young people build on their strengths, rather than be overly focused on what they can't do well, or at all. The work is deeply satisfying. I am part of a high-functioning team of professionals who work effectively together to operate the center and support the teens, and who trust each other to do our individual work in teaching, mentoring, and supporting the teens to live their lives. I am thrilled to be taking direct, grassroots action to demonstrate how teens can be trusted to self-direct their own educations.

9

Common Questions

When I first learned about North Star and the idea of noncompulsory, noncoercive, self-directed learning, I was excited by the idea, but I had absolutely zero frame of reference for how it worked in practice. I was traditionally educated; I worked in traditional schools, as did my parents, wife, and other friends and family; and I thought about the role of the teacher, the structure of the day, the curriculum, and everything else in a traditional way.

So while I was enthusiastic and wanted to learn more about North Star and how it worked, I had a lot of questions for Kenneth and looked at the program from a traditional mindset. Even after I started working at PLC, I had to go through a deschooling process myself as I learned to let go of a lot of the assumptions built into the traditional model. In fact, I remember one day early in my first year on staff at PLC when I was watching the teens playing on their computers, sitting and talking, not doing anything that would have counted as "work" in school. My anxiety level started rising rapidly, and I thought to myself, *What are we doing here? What is the worth or value of this? Have we made a terrible mistake?* I'm sure this is very similar to what many of the PLC parents feel at the beginning. I hadn't deschooled yet. I pulled out my notebook and wrote down a list called "What I Need to Keep in Mind When I Get Frustrated." Here it is from that day in 2011:

- It is not my life or education. It is theirs. My role is to support it but not control it.

- The pace of learning is uneven. They may do nothing one day and amazing things the next.
- Sometimes people are tired or don't feel well or have a bad day.
- Academic achievement is not always the most important thing in a child's life at any given moment.
- Kids don't learn much at school. Is their life and learning better <u>in fact</u> as opposed to an idealized version of what school could have been for them?
- What does not seem like learning, can be.
- Skills of independence and self-directedness take time and a lot of failure. The process cannot be short-cutted.
- Keep your eyes on the long-term goal. Think big picture.

I'd probably add some and edit others, but these ideas helped me get perspective on what I was trying to do as a staff member at PLC as opposed to being a teacher.

Here are some of the common questions we get from teachers and others interested in the model and how we respond to them.

DON'T YOU NEED A HIGH SCHOOL DIPLOMA TO GET ANYWHERE IN LIFE?

This is a little-known fact of the American educational system: most often you do not need any kind of diploma to do what you want to do in life, including go to college. This flies in the face of what most people have heard repeated over and over again (stay in school!) so some more explanation might be helpful.

Let me back up a little bit.

It is absolutely never necessary to attend, complete, and graduate from a high school to move onto whatever next steps you want. There are certain schools, programs, or jobs that might require some kind of state-issued diploma, but this requirement can always be satisfied by taking the GED or, depending on the state, other degree-granting tests like the HiSET.

Typically, though, a high school diploma is not an admissions requirement for many colleges. No one checks if you have a diploma if you want to start your own business, and if an employer requires a diploma, you can either have a homeschooling diploma so you can check the box on the application or you can take the GED. In New Jersey, there is even a program where you can submit thirty hours of college credits to the state at any point in your life and they issue you a high school diploma. Many people are shocked to know that a high school diploma is simply not required for admission to even the elite colleges like Princeton University. Obviously, their admissions criteria are not easy, and you have to be doing some pretty amazing things to be accepted, but graduating from high school is not one of them.

Our members take a couple of potential paths after PLC if they plan to go to college. First is to start getting involved at the community college when they are sixteen, seventeen, or eighteen and take a class or two at a time. They can accumulate enough credits to be considered a college student transfer to a four-year university, in which case what they did or did not do in high school essentially becomes irrelevant. Any sort of diploma is typically unnecessary and standardized tests like the SAT also become irrelevant. This makes sense. One of the justifications for high school and the SAT is to prepare you for and prove that you can do college level work. If you start taking college classes earlier and are successful in them, that is all the proof many colleges are looking for.

Community colleges are open enrollment schools, which means they do not have entrance requirements other than perhaps placement testing. In practice, that means teens can take all the time they want to explore and try out various paths even if those paths have zero relation to the typical academic path college-bound students take, and college is still a very real option for them. As Kenneth from North Star likes to say, a teen can take four years and do nothing but go into the woods and build huts, and the second that teen decides that he or she wants to go to college, the teen can walk into the community college and start. Close to one-third of the graduating class of the large suburban high school I taught at started at the local community college with plans to either stay there or transfer in a year or two. Teens can do way more interesting things with their lives than high school and still end up in the same exact spot as many of their friends who attend high school.

Another path forward is applying directly to a four-year school as a homeschooler. In this situation, teens apply on the strength of what they did during what would be considered their high school career. Perhaps at one time college admissions people raised their eyebrows at homeschool applications, but by now, with millions of kids in the United States homeschooling, the path from homeschool to college is well worn. Every college we have seen has homeschooling application procedures.

The basic difference when applying to college as a homeschooler is that instead of the high school doing the documentation and keeping track of what the child is learning, that responsibility falls to the family, with PLC's support. We document the types of learning each member does and then when the times comes to apply to college, we translate it into a form that colleges are familiar with, most often a narrative transcript. We also encourage our members to keep a list of books they have read, as many colleges will ask that of homeschoolers. You can see an example of this type of narrative transcript in the appendix.

When documenting, we like to think of courses as buckets that get filled with learning opportunities in which the member participated. One of the great advantages of homeschooling is that these courses don't need to look like traditional equivalents in high school; they can still satisfy the admissions requirements for college and can be based on the interests and strengths of each child. For example, a course like English 9, which would be the freshman year language arts course, doesn't have to consist of working through a big textbook or sticky noting novels to death. It can include a wide range of activities and classes based on language. So the English 9 bucket could include a one hour a week fiction writing class at PLC, plays the teen has seen throughout the year, a book club at the library or at PLC the teen joined, a stack of books the teen read independently, a collection of short stories the teen wrote and self-published, a fan fiction he or she posted online, lyrics to songs the teen writes, a travel journal he or she kept of a family vacation. The possibilities are endless.

You take all of these activities, put a course called English 9 on the homeschooling transcript, and then write up a narrative of what this course included, noting the books the teen has read and the writing he or she has done. If I'm an admissions counselor and I'm looking at two applicants, the first of which went to traditional school, did the run-of-the-mill language classes, and got a B+ in English 9 and an A in English 10 through 12 while the second is someone who has self-published his or her own novel or collection of short-stories, I'm interested in knowing more about the second candidate. Every course can be a collection of cool activities, learning, and even formal classes and be based on the individuality of each teen.

Some schools require standardized testing like the SAT or ACT for homeschoolers, especially if they have not spent any time in a traditional school or community college. We help kids prepare for those tests if the schools they are applying to require them. The big message, however, is that it is not necessary to attend traditional high school to get into the college you want. I recommend looking at any college's admissions page and you will find information on what it takes to apply as a homeschooler. Every PLC member who has wanted to go to college has, many of them to their first-choice school.

This is a sampling of the colleges that North Star and PLC members have been accepted into as of 2016: Miami University (Ohio), Colorado College, Hampshire College, University of Colorado, UMass Amherst, University of the Arts, University of California Santa Cruz, Union College, Marlboro College, Columbia College Chicago, Savannah College of Art and Design, Prescott College, Lewis and Clark, University of North Texas, Wilson College, Pitzer College, Cazenovia College, Warren Wilson College, University of Vermont, University of Montana, Cairn University, The Relativity School, Rider University, Rutgers University, Amherst College, Antioch College, Art Institute of Boston, Bard College, Bennington College, Brandeis University, Brown University, Bryn Mawr College, Colorado State University, Columbia University, Earlham College, Fashion Institute of Technology, Haverford College, Ithaca College, Northeastern University, Sarah Lawrence College, Smith College, Texas A&M University, University of Massachusetts, University of Alaska, University of Auckland, Wellesley College, and Williams College.

IF YOU DON'T MAKE KIDS DO SOMETHING, WON'T THEY DO NOTHING?

This is perhaps the biggest fear people have about self-directed, noncoercive education for teens: If we don't force kids to do things like math or writing, there is no way they will choose to do things that aren't "fun." Instead, they will spend their time sitting on the couch, watching YouTube videos or playing video games.

This aspect of our work, to me, is by far the most interesting and challenging part. There are a lot of things to say about it that are subtle and nuanced and very often tied to the specific teen and his or her specific situation.

First, every teen reacts to this newfound freedom to direct his or her own life and learning differently, and the reactions are not that different from those of adults when they leave a job they don't like or retire. Sometimes just removing the stress, anxiety, and mountains of required work at school does the trick. We work with some kids who are so overjoyed by the prospects of getting to learn anything they want, however they want and have control over their own time that they dive into everything immediately and create this wonderful, rich, and full life. In those situations, we just get out of the way, help where we can, and make contacts to programs and opportunities we think they would enjoy. If anything, the problem in these cases is that their lives are overfull and they need to scale it back a bit to stay sane and not run themselves into the ground. The easy part is always the academic side of things. If a young person is interested in physics and is motivated to learn it, there are about a million resources and things he or she can do to learn about physics; it is simply a process of pointing him or her in the right direction.

Another common reaction is for the young people to try to replicate what they "should" be doing if they were in school. They see what all of their friends who are still in school are doing and feel some obligation to continue with that plan, even though it is not required and is not coming from their own interests and desires. Oftentimes they will fill up their time with a number of classes that mostly replicate what is happening in school. As they get used to the idea of directing their own time and figuring out their own paths, they start to scale back some of these classes and start filling their time with activities that are more in line with their emerging sense of what they want in their lives. It might be more time for self-directed activities or self-study, more time to spend with friends, different classes, or time volunteering or working. This process of learning what opportunities to say no to is a critical skill in any balanced life, and our members have a chance to start practicing that in a very real and concrete way much earlier than most young people.

Another common reaction to leaving the traditional system, especially if the teen has had a hard school experience, is the dreaded *do nothing* option. This isn't as common as people imagine, but it does happen, and it is the most challenging situation to work in, but at the same time also the most rewarding. We often call this period the detox phase or the deschooling phase, and it can look like a lot of things, but very often it looks like the teen sitting on the couch, watching YouTube videos or Netflix, texting friends, Snapchatting, or playing video games for a good portion of each day. This can often last months.

There are a lot of different ways kids can end up here. They might have been totally stressed out and filled with anxiety in school and they simply need a break and time to recover, or they might have associated learning (exciting) with school (not so exciting) and they know I didn't like school so therefore I must not like learning too. Or they could be dealing with more serious issues like depression. Either way, the outward appearance is of a teen doing nothing.

We work with teens in a couple of ways during the deschooling period. The first is to simply pay attention to them. Even though they may be sitting on the couch most of the time, we still talk and interact with them. Hopefully they form some connections with other teens and chat with them. We also invite them to play games that get organized as well as reach out and have mentoring meetings with them to talk about how they are doing and if there is anything we could be helping them with. What is critical to understand is that we are not a school and therefore we do not judge our success strictly by academic measures.

Our goal is not to get kids into traditional academic classes as fast as possible. We are able to work with teens where they are at and on what they need at that moment in their lives, and that's rarely Algebra II. In fact, forcing kids into academic situations when they are not ready is counterproductive. Not only are they not going to learn anything, but the added stress distracts them from the real work they need to be doing on themselves. It also damages the mentoring relationship that the staff wants to have with those young people. We go from trusted partner and mentor to just another adult trying to get a kid to do things he or she doesn't want to do. Young people need the time and space to figure out what they want in life and then the support to have the confidence to go after it.

Almost universally at some point, kids who are metaphorically "on the couch" start getting involved in activities, finding interests, and taking steps toward their adult lives. Some do it more quickly than others, and to be honest, some kids never get through it while they are with us; their challenges are just too great.

If you talk with kids who have come through the other side of the do-nothing phase, they often will tell you that the recovery period was the most important time for them. When you strip away all the required formalities and apparent "busyness" of a typical school schedule, you are confronted by three questions almost daily: who am I?; what do I want?; and what do I want to do with my time?. We feel it is much better to do this contemplation when you are a teenager as opposed to not confronting those questions until much later in life. Most kids eventually realize that sitting on the couch, watching cat videos on YouTube, or playing video games day after day is not a very inspiring life. This is the goal—to help young people take responsibility for their lives and realize that their lives are their own and will be what they make of them. It is nearly impossible to bribe, threaten, or coerce people to come to this realization, so allowing people to have their own process on their own timeline is important to us.

What also happens in these situations is that while one teen is in the deschooling phase, many teens are not detoxing and are already working on making a life for themselves. Kids pay attention. They see people at PLC getting their driver's licenses, applying to college, getting jobs or internships, having money in their pockets, talking about the classes and tutors they have at PLC, and taking community college courses. They realize that they want those things too. We are also constantly bringing new opportunities to the group—new volunteers, new trips, new workshops—and encouraging our teens to try them to see if anything lights a spark.

Many people feel like an all-voluntary educational setting means that teens have zero accountability in their lives. This is not true. PLC members are accountable to themselves and their future goals. If they want to get into college, as many of them do, they have to pay at least some attention to the admissions requirements like English and math. They are accountable to their families. They are accountable to their workplaces if they have jobs or are volunteering. They are accountable to the staff and volunteers they work with at PLC; it is not good to just blow people off when you have made a commitment.

The key difference between traditional schools and a self-directed learning center is that the responsibility and accountability are self-chosen instead of imposed externally. When I was a teacher and talked about my students' "responsibility" to get the work in on time, what I really was looking for was compliance to the requirement I set for them. Real responsibility is following through on commitments freely chosen, not simply doing what you're told. There is a crucial difference there.

Of course, some teens struggle with issues deeper than just not liking school or what a change of context can solve. Some never form relationships with the adults at PLC or other members and never get fully hooked into the community. Not everyone thrives in a self-directed learning environment, but we have seen that for most kids, it can have a powerful influence and allows young people to create a life they couldn't imagine before.

HOW LONG ARE MEMBERS USUALLY INVOLVED?

There are a couple of fairly typical arcs that our members follow in terms of when they join and how long they are with us. The first consists of teens who join during what would be their middle school years. Seventh and eighth grade is the best time to try an alternative educational path if someone just wants to see what it is like. That's because if it doesn't work out, there are very simple ways to integrate back into the traditional system.

No one really cares what you do or do not do during seventh and eighth grade. There is no certification or diploma that is given to certify that you have completed those grades. So if you are homeschooling for eighth grade and you decide you want try high school, you just register, they stick you in ninth grade, and away you go—no problem. We've had members over the years whose plan all along was to do homeschooling through junior high and then transition back to a traditional high school. We celebrate and support this choice, and it generally has worked out really well for everyone involved.

If you are already in high school, decide to homeschool for tenth grade, and then want to go back for eleventh grade, that is when things get a bit more complicated. You can certainly do that, and the public schools are required by law to take you back, but it is totally up to them what they give you credit for from your time homeschooling. They could choose not to give you any credits for "tenth" grade, and you may end up having to take sophomore and junior classes to catch up to their credit requirements for graduation. We have had members successfully petition to get credit for work done while homeschooling, but it was for accredited work they did at the community college or on advanced placement tests that they took and passed.

Perhaps the most usual arc our members take is to complete their freshman year of high school even if it is a struggle. Then the hope is that tenth grade will be better. When they get to tenth grade, they realize it is very much like ninth grade and not better at all, and so around December or January, they find us and call. They might be full-time with us for the rest of their tenth-grade year, full-time all of the next year, and then for what would be their "senior" year start being more involved with the community college or working and have our support part-time. We've had a couple of members go to the local technical high school part-time for their senior year because they are able to enroll in community college classes in various specific programs tuition-free and then be with us part-time.

It is rare for us to have someone with us full-time from day one of what would be high school all the way through to the last day of "senior" year. We like this because it typically means our members are out there making a life for themselves and don't need us as much anymore. It seems counter-intuitive perhaps, but our goal is to help kids not need us anymore and be independent.

WHAT MIGHT A TYPICAL WEEK OR DAY LOOK LIKE FOR A TEEN AT A SELF-DIRECTED LEARNING CENTER?

I'm not sure there is a typical day or week because our members' experiences are very personalized and based on their interests and where they are in their lives at the moment. I'll take one fairly active member and detail what her week looks like.

Each morning she participates in an aerobics class before arriving at PLC. On Monday at PLC, she does Current Events at 9:00 a.m. and then has the 10:00 a.m. block free. Sometimes she works on an online geometry class during this time, but she might also be studying for her driver's permit test, hanging around with other kids, or playing a game. We do our mentoring meeting at 11:00 a.m. and then she is free at noon and will sometimes walk up to the shopping center with other kids to get lunch. At 1:00 p.m. she is in the Do Something class, which is a social activism class, and then has 2:00 p.m. free to work on other things or socialize.

On Tuesday, she chooses to do the later aerobics class so she can get a bit more sleep and arrives at PLC about the time our all-group meeting starts around 10:00 a.m. Then she does an environmental sustainability class at 11:00 a.m., followed by lunch. At 1:00 p.m. it is Essay Writing followed by Beginner Spanish at 2:00 p.m. On Tuesday nights she participates in a calligraphy art class from 7:00 to 8:30 p.m.

On Wednesdays when we are closed, she does aerobics in the morning and then has a shift as a receptionist at a local eye-care center for three hours. For Thursday, she has a one-on-one art tutor at 9:00 a.m. and then Early American History at 10:00 a.m. Then she has in succession Gender Studies, a writing one-on-one with a Princeton University student, a class called Be More Awesomer in which we try to work on being our best selves, and she then is involved in a short six-week course on personality tests and career planning.

On Fridays when the rest of PLC is taking trips or having workshops, she has decided to pick up another shift at the eye center. She plays tennis on Saturday afternoons. Sprinkled throughout her week is drawing, working on Spanish with Duolingo, doing some personal writing, taking an online class for geometry, and researching art-based summer camps for this year.

These are just the scheduled activities that she participates in, but there are also lots of spontaneous games and activities that come up throughout the week. She has also tried a number of different classes or activities that are on the calendar at PLC, but she has settled into this particular mix for the time being. It would look completely different for each member of PLC. We have some members who participate in almost no scheduled classes but maybe do a couple of one-on-one sessions and their mentoring meeting or otherwise do self-study, work on a business, or do their art. There are also members who are involved at the community college and might only be at PLC half the time we are open. It really depends on the member and where that teen is at in his or her life and education.

IF EVERYTHING IS VOLUNTARY, HOW ARE KIDS EXPOSED TO THINGS THAT THEY DON'T KNOW ABOUT AND MIGHT NOT VOLUNTARILY TRY, BUT MIGHT LOVE IF GIVEN A CHANCE?

When it comes to simple exposure, PLC members have the opportunity to be exposed to a lot of things. Our calendar has classes and tutorials based on the interests of about thirty teens (and close to an equal number of adults) with diverse interests. As I write, the calendar has activities ranging from digital recording to existentialism to Japanese to intro programming to technical writing. We encourage our members, especially at the beginning of the year, to experiment and try out as many of these activities as possible before deciding what they want to stick with.

PLC also takes advantage of the community around us. We take trips to local businesses or museums, among other things. Sometimes these trips spark an interest in someone. The most recent example was our trip to a recording studio in Philadelphia that got some of our members considering a career in sound engineering. We invite community members to offer one-time work-shops on Fridays as well. This has ranged from an emergency room nurse to an organic farmer to an expert coffee roaster. This is a routine and planned part of PLC, so the number and variety of different types of exposure kids can have is fairly impressive. When I compare this to the real life exposure most of my high school students had, it's not really a contest.

When I reflect on how I came to love the things I enjoy doing in my own life, I don't believe any of them developed because someone forced me to do it initially. What it really came down to for me was the importance of the relationships I had with people and my subsequent openness to the things they liked because I respected them. My love of Frank Zappa, for example, would not have happened if I hadn't respected and enjoyed hanging around and playing guitar with one of the older guys I worked with in a factory over the summers during college. The relationship came first and the openness to trying new things came second. If someone had sat me down and forced me to listen to a bunch of crazy Frank Zappa recordings and then tested and graded me on how well I had learned the music of Frank Zappa, I don't think I would still be listening to him today.

The History of Western Music class I was required to take in college is a good example. I'm not listening to much Gregorian chant music today even though I'm sure parts of it are beautiful and sublime. I don't think the ability to name drop Gregorian chant was worth four months of my time. I'm not sure this type of forced exposure really progresses past the superficial level of familiarity in most cases.

DON'T KIDS NEED STRUCTURE AND SUPERVISION?

Yes, although we might reframe both words a little bit. We feel like each young person thrives in different situations, so the amount of structure necessary depends on the child. We work with some kids who want everything laid out in front of them: they want a full schedule and want to know what they are doing from hour to hour. Some PLC members are in a scheduled and organized activity almost every second they are with us each week. That works incredibly well for some kids.

We have other kids who wither under that kind of structure. They thrive having greater personal control over their time. They want to go read a book under a tree when it is nice out from 10:17 a.m. until they are finished with the chapter at 12:33 p.m., and then they want to come in and work on their drawing from 1:46 p.m. until they finish the background at 2:44 p.m. Cramming their schedules full of classes actually gets in the way of their learning and growth, and they don't want that.

The point is that there can be as much structure or as little structure as you want in a self-directed learning environment. It is just that there is no externally imposed structure by the organization. Often kids will find a balance between the two extremes. Parents might expect that they take a certain amount of classes and scheduled activities (they are paying for *something*, after all) but then are happy to support the teens in having significant amounts of downtime during which they can hang out with friends, go for walks, or work on their own projects.

Thinking about and being intentional with how you spend your time is one of the greatest skills anyone can learn in his or her life, and in self-directed learning centers, this is practiced on a daily basis.

In terms of supervision, we feel the trend in modern parenting has been to go to the extreme of supervision to the point of control. This is not really healthy for the parents or for their children's growth into adulthood. Almost anyone over the age of thirty-five can recall a time when they were sent out to play with neighborhood friends with no cell phone and no way to really be in touch with their parents; they were just told to be back when the street lights came on. Kids enjoyed a huge amount of unstructured, unsupervised free time. This allowed them time to negotiate and resolve their own disagreements, find ways to amuse themselves rather than being passive consumers of entertainment, and organize games as opposed to being in adult-led youth sports programs. We feel that, in contrast to supervision, children really need trust, time, and support. They need adults who are involved in their lives and who they can come to for advice and support but who don't look to control their time or fix all their problems for them (see "When Helping Isn't Helpful" in chapter 10).

WITHOUT TESTS AND GRADES, HOW WILL WE KNOW IF THEY ARE LEARNING ANYTHING?

I would like to turn this question around just a bit: Even with tests and grades, how do we know they learn anything? Think about classes in traditional schools with tests and quizzes and projects. How many kids that you work with, even the ones who get good grades, really learn something that they retain and that impacts their lives? How many of them play the game, fill out the worksheets on time, memorize for the tests, do well, and then immediately forget everything after the A comes back on the paper? I led a number of honors classes when I taught at the high school. How much US History that we discussed in class would they remember and be able to intelligibly talk about three days after the final exam? Maybe five to ten percent?

These were the students that by all traditional measures excelled in school and would say that they enjoyed my class. Imagine kids who don't excel at school and don't really like or care much about their classes. How much are they learning even if they are passing the class? How much time is wasted in this way? Paraphrasing John Holt, learning is a product of the activity of the learner, not the activity of the teacher.

We really only learn and retain what we are interested in or find useful anyway, regardless of how great the lessons are or how wonderful the resources. So at PLC, we feel that the best way to support real learning and growth is to start not with some externally created curriculum that may or may not be related to the child's real interests, but with the child's strengths, abilities, and interests. Then we build from there.

Many of the classes are very small at PLC, and there is a lot of one-on-one tutoring that happens. So while we don't have tests and quizzes to "assess" learning, it becomes apparent pretty quickly through conversation and body language if someone is "getting it" or not. It also comes through in the teen's actions and behavior. I have a number of parents tell me that their kids will come home and talk to them about what is going on in the news after our current events class. Or a young person who has been watching photography tutorials on YouTube will start taking improved photographs. Or another teen in the evolution class will start reading books on their own about evolution.

Sometimes kids have to submit to more traditional measures in the pursuit of their goals: the SAT for some colleges, GED tests, community college placement tests, etc. We even have some members who like to have tests and quizzes given in their classes at PLC, and they will request them. For example, a teen working through an Algebra textbook with a tutor might like to take the end of section quizzes to figure out if they really know the material. That is fine with us as long as the teen is choosing that and it works best for them. It is used strictly as an aid in learning and not in an institutional sense of judging or ranking young people's learning.

WHAT HAPPENS WHEN KIDS MOVE ON TO MORE TRADITIONAL AND STRUCTURED LEARNING ENVIRONMENTS LIKE COLLEGE? DON'T THEY STRUGGLE WITH THE STRUCTURE AND REQUIREMENTS?

Self-directed learning seems so far outside the norm of the traditional school system and workplace that many people wonder if kids who are used to directing their time and efforts can adapt to suddenly having to take direction and meet externally created goals like you would find in a typical job or college classroom. The answer is yes, given that the young person wants what is on offer. The critical thing to look at is not the course or job requirements but the context. If teens choose to put themselves into a job or more structured learning environment because they want it and it is on the path to something else they want, then often the details of how it is structured are irrelevant. They will do whatever it takes to make it happen, provided that they are there for the right reasons and they see a purpose in it.

For example, we had one member in Princeton who was very smart and funny and awesome in a lot of ways, but he was basically failing out of Princeton High School. It was not because the material was too hard in a general sense but rather that he saw no meaning in the work he was being asked to do, and the stress and anxiety from mountains of homework was shutting him down. He came to PLC halfway through his sophomore year and was with us full- or part-time until he would have been a "senior." If you had asked me what kind of academic work he did while he was at PLC, I would say spotty at best. He did a little math, a little bit of US History, a smidgen of database design, and Spanish, but certainly nothing sustained or regular. What he did have at PLC, however, was the time, space, and support to figure out what he wanted in life and start taking steps toward what he wanted.

He very much wanted to be a first-responder, perhaps police, fire, or EMT. After he got through the initial detox phase, he started doing things in small ways that would point directly toward his future life. He created a position at PLC called the first aid and safety manager. He got a first-aid box like those used on ambulances and researched all the materials that should go in there. He was creating purchase orders and tracking how much it would cost to get all the supplies. He studied a little database design so that he could make a system to track injury incidents at PLC. Any time someone got a cut, there he would be putting on the latex gloves, disinfecting and bandaging the wound, and then making an incident report that would go into his database. People would slip down our stairs when it would rain, so out he went to get weather stripping for the stairs.

He also created something called the Princeton Airsoft Rifle Team, which was sort of like paintball but a bit more serious. He created an application form for people who wanted to be part of the team, and they would hold trainings and go compete on the weekends. He started volunteering at the fire station, too. How much world history, trigonometry, or writing did he do while at PLC? Almost none. From one view you could say that he was wasting his time compared to his peers in school who were doing hour after hour of academic work and that this should have put him at a disadvantage when it came to a future career and in life. What he was really doing, however, was absolutely the most critical thing that he could have been doing to help himself get where he wanted to go. He was almost play acting what he wanted to do when he grew up, learning leadership, and figuring out what he wanted to do with his life.

His "senior" year, he decided he wanted to enroll in the fire science program at the local community college. The classes he would have to take would be structured very much like the ones he was failing in Princeton High School just eighteen months earlier. There would be required reading material, tests to be taken, grades to be earned, and papers to write.

He was the top student in all of his classes.

What changed? What had PLC done to make this possible? From an intellectual standpoint, nothing had changed. He was still the same person with all the same innate abilities. We taught him no special techniques, no study skills, no revolutionary way to write A+ papers. What had changed dramatically, however, was the context in which he was attending those classes. He had chosen to be there for his own reasons and to help him get where he wanted to go. The difference this makes cannot be overstated.

When he was at Princeton High School, the classes and learning were being forced upon him in a way that was detrimental to his intellectual and personal growth. As opposed to high school being a four-year opportunity to learn and develop, it turned into a four-year prison sentence. When he enrolled in the fire science classes, he chose to be there. It was directly related to his vision for his life. He cared about the material he was being exposed to, and he realized that even though he might not like aspects of the work or the structure, his performance in these classes was a critical step in doing the thing that he wanted to do. This makes all the difference. Recently, he was accepted as a transfer student to Rider University as well as Rutgers University in their public safety program.

We find that if someone is really interested in something and truly wants that experience, the structure of the class is rarely the deciding factor of how well that person does. Sure, if someone struggles at reading, a class with hundreds of pages to read will still be a challenge. But if they want it badly enough and are willing to ask for help and support, young people will find a way to do the things they want to do.

DOES THIS REALLY WORK? WHAT ARE THE LONG-TERM RESULTS FOR THE TEENS?

If you step back and look at homeschooling in general, the answer is, "Yes, this works." Homeschoolers go to college, start businesses, have families, raise children, and have life outcomes very similar to people who stayed in school. There is no doubt about that. There are not a huge number of academic studies look-ing at homeschooling (and especially at self-directed learning in particular), but if you're interested, there is a selected list in the appendix of this book.

The long-term results for teens who join self-directed learning centers like PLC or North Star are basically the same as the results for homeschoolers in general. They have jobs ranging from lawyer to yoga instructor to superinten-dent of a local school system. They go to colleges ranging from small liberal arts schools to large public colleges to elite universities like Brown or MIT. What we say to our families is that choosing to homeschool does not close any doors that would otherwise be open to you. Everything you can imagine wanting out of life is possible through homeschooling, and our programs sim-ply support families to do homeschooling well and provide opportunities they might have trouble finding on their own.

WHAT KIND OF FAMILY SUPPORT IS NEEDED FOR THIS TO WORK? WHEN IS IT NOT A GOOD FIT FOR FAMILIES?

The short answer is the more support, the better, as is generally the case in any kind of educational setting. PLC has worked with all kinds of families that offer very different levels of support and involvement. We have worked with single parents who basically just drop their children off and pick them up and are not very involved. We have worked with families that are divorced and one parent is more supportive of PLC and homeschooling than the other. We work with families where both parents are heavily involved and might even volunteer or be on our board of trustees. It really just depends on the situa-tion. At a bare minimum, families need to commit to getting the teen to PLC regularly, put some resources toward paying our fees, and come in for family meetings about three times a year so they have a sense of what their children are up to and what the next steps might be.

We have definitely had situations when the lack of family support has made it hard to have good outcomes. It is also hard when the family is not really on board with the philosophy of self-directed learning and is looking for us to be a school for their child and force them do certain things or study particular topics.

I would also say that we have not been successful in situations in which a teen had a serious drug or alcohol issue or where the teen's depression or anxiety was so severe that he or she needed much more specialized support than we could offer.

WHY SHOULD A FAMILY PAY YOU A LOT OF MONEY INSTEAD OF HOMESCHOOLING INDEPENDENTLY?

Families shouldn't join or pay us anything unless they want to. We always make sure to let families know that homeschooling is free, that they can do it independently of us, as most homeschoolers do, and that they can start tomorrow regardless if they join PLC or not. That is part of the revolutionary aspect of homeschooling. Anyone can do it at any time.

The reason we feel PLC is worth every penny is because many families don't feel like they can take on the responsibility of homeschooling by themselves. We provide what I believe is an amazing amount of personalized academic and nonacademic support for them to take this leap and have a much better situation for their children, who might be struggling in school. We also provide a ready-made community for their teenager, which is a bit more difficult to find as an independent homeschooler, but it is certainly possible.

DON'T KIDS NEED TRAINED PROFESSIONAL TEACHERS?

I would suggest that young people need interesting, inspiring, and helpful adults to support them and that this is independent of any sort of credentialing system. We all know certified teachers who are amazing and inspiring and change young people's lives. We all also know certified teachers who are mediocre. And we all know people who went through the training and are certified teachers but who have no business being around children. It is not the piece of paper that makes teachers great; it is their unique personalities, their enthusiasm for their subject and life, and their ability to make connections and form relationships with young people. You can find these people in every walk of life: there are architects who are amazing teachers, mechanics who are amazing teachers, and professional teachers who are amazing teachers.

As I mentioned previously, at PLC our full-time paid staff do not spend the majority of their time actually teaching content. I lead maybe four hours worth of classes each week. The majority of my time is spent mentoring young people, building relationships with families, and looking after the administrative needs of the center. We have volunteers and university students lead the majority of our classes, and almost none of them have teaching certificates. This typically works because they have a deep interest in the classes they are leading and the young people who come to the classes are interested to learn what they have to offer. So even if they are not the best at presenting or simplifying material, our volunteers generally do well because most of our classes are very small—in the three to six people range. Volunteers who really are not able to work with young people don't stay around very long because everything is optional. If our teen members aren't getting what they want out of a relationship with a volunteer, they can gracefully end their involvement and then the volunteer won't have anyone to work with.

My experience in college training to become a teacher was not particularly useful and often irrelevant to the work I ended up doing. It was a lot of how to control a classroom, how to write lesson plans, how to deal with curriculum and state standards, and how to create and score tests. Much of what I learned about teaching and connecting with young people came from actually doing the work. So much of what teachers are trained to do becomes irrelevant in self-directed learning centers, and the rest can be learned in a matter of weeks on the job. Great teachers need freedom to be creative and to connect with young people in memorable ways, which is not the situation in most traditionally structured schools.

So yes, we need highly skilled and caring adults to work with kids, but they don't need to have a teaching certificate.

ISN'T THIS ELITIST PRIVATE EDUCATION THAT WILL UNDERCUT PUBLIC SCHOOLS AND LEAVE LOW-INCOME CHILDREN BEHIND?

Self-directed learning centers don't undercut public schools any more than other educational options like Catholic schools or other private schools. They are not charter schools that pull their budgets out of the money designated for our public schools. PLC is privately funded through membership fees and dona-tions. I believe strongly that there should be public money to support the educa-tion of all children in the United States, and many of the families at PLC believe the same and use the public school system for their other children. Somehow we have developed a public system that essentially uses one educational model that doesn't necessarily work for all children. It would be great if public money could be used to support self-directed learning options and make them free for the families that need them. Perhaps the growing movement of families away from traditionally structured public schools will spur change to a more noncoercive, interest-based style of education in public schools, or at least create a school within a school that will utilize this approach. In the meantime, establishing these kinds of programs outside the traditional model is critical to helping a large segment of children get an appropriate education that will work for them.

We don't see self-directed learning as solely an elitist movement for the wealthy who can afford to pull their children from public schools. Certainly like every other organization, nonprofit, or business, we need to have members who can pay our fees to cover our expenses, but every center in the Liberated Learners network thus far has built it into its core principles that they will not turn families away solely based on an inability to pay the full fees. At PLC, we offer about one-third of our operating budget as fee reductions to make sure that we have an economically diverse membership. Some families pay our full fees, and some families can't, and don't, pay anything near our full fees. Then we attempt to fundraise to make up some of this difference. It is not easy to make that financial model work, but we have done reasonably well.

WHAT ABOUT SPECIAL NEEDS KIDS OR CHILDREN WITH LEARNING DIFFERENCES?

Self-directed learning centers are not explicitly therapeutic programs. Typically the staff do not have specialized training. Because of our structure, members have to be able to care for themselves and not be a potential danger to them-selves or others. If a family has concerns about what their child would do if left unsupervised or walking into town by him or herself or with a group of kids, a self-directed learning center might not be the right environment for them.

It is very rare that we ask a family to terminate their membership, but it has happened. In one case, the child needed much more specialized support and intensive care than our model could provide. In another, the child got into trouble when he or she was off the grounds of PLC and the teen was not willing to make changes to prevent it from happening again or mitigate the damage it could do to the program, and they essentially chose to leave the community.

That being said, how we operate and the structure of the program often results in what would be called therapeutic outcomes and often includes what would be put in an individualized educational program (IEP) in traditional schools. If a child has a lot of anxiety around the amount of homework or stress school places on him or her and this manifests in physical or mental health issues, coming to a relaxed place like PLC helps tremendously. Almost all the classes and activities at PLC are very small and personalized, so teens with learning differences can have the experience tailored to their particular needs and they can move at their own pace.

I found that many of the accommodations children received in school were either pointless (preferential seating, etc.) or were solely interested in improving grades and not necessarily about learning (test retakes, eliminating choices on multiple choice tests, etc.)

Also, given the flexible structure at PLC, kids don't have to sit still all day. If they need to get up and walk around the room for a moment during class, that is not a problem. They can go for a hike in the middle of the day to clear their heads if needed. Kids can really find a rhythm and structure that works for them, and this often takes care of a lot of problems they were having in school.

We have worked successfully with children who have dyslexia or were on the autism spectrum. If their needs are more than we can accommodate, sometimes they will work with an outside reading specialist or therapist, but typically a diagnosis does not prevent someone from joining a self-directed learning center.

HOW DO YOU DEAL WITH DISCIPLINE PROBLEMS?

Compared with when I worked in a public or private high school, PLC has remarkably fewer discipline problems. I think this is because most of the things that cause children to act out in school are absent in a self-directed learning environment. There is no one to rebel against. No one is telling you to do things you don't want to do or to take your hat off or put your phone away. Kids have freedom of movement and don't feel trapped. They can move around, or if they are having a bad day, they are not forced to sit through class after class with their tension and stress rising each minute.

The relationship staff have with the members is one of care, respect, and concern. When problems arise, we don't deal with them in punishment mode. There are no suspensions or detentions or anything of the sort. We work to help people see the consequences their actions have on themselves and others in the community and then we work to repair relationships that might have been damaged.

When problems do come up, they are typically minor and of the interpersonal variety: someone said something about someone else behind his or her back or online, someone was messing with someone's stuff, two people just really don't like each other and words are exchanged. Thankfully we have never had an all-out physical fight.

We deal with issues that come up in a couple of ways, all of them trying to respect everyone in the situation and find a resolution that keeps the sense of community and caring intact. First, we encourage kids to deal with the issues that arise on their own. If someone messes with your stuff or says something you find disparaging, say something to the person and see if it can be resolved right then and there. If it is an ongoing issue that they have attempted to deal with but still continues, they can call a staff member into a meeting with the other person and we'll try to mediate the conflict: what is happening, what impact is it having, how can we find a way to be together in this space? Most of the issues we deal with never go beyond this. If it is a specific and ongoing issue with a particular member, we will often deal with it in our mentoring meetings: "I've noticed you've been doing this and it seems like it is having this negative impact. Do you see that too? Is there a particular reason why it is happening? What could be done differently?"

If there is a pervasive issue in the community that is not tied to an individual, we will often bring it up in our all-group meeting that happens each week.

We would never call out a single person, but it might be a problem with groups of people hanging out in some of the rooms in an exclusive, unwelcoming way that feels cliquish. Or it might be a sense that gossiping is prevalent in the community. If there is an incident that really causes alarm, we might set up a meeting with the member and his or her parents to just stress the seriousness of the situation and try to enlist their help in resolving it. As a very last resort, we might ask someone to leave the community, but it would have to be for some major incident or ongoing behavior that would likely be criminal in nature.

The real dividing line here is that the staff has to feel confident and trust the members. If I wouldn't trust a member enough to leave my computer or phone on a table while I go to the bathroom or run to the bank for a couple of minutes, that is an issue.

The best way to deal with discipline issues is to create a respectful culture at the center that is safe and welcoming so that it preempts a lot of problems before they arise. A good culture communicates what is acceptable and not acceptable in the community without having to enforce rules or deal out punishment. That is what we strive for and talk about with the members on a regular basis.

ISN'T HOMESCHOOLING JUST FOR ULTRA-DEVOUT CHRISTIANS OR KIDS WHO CAN'T "HACK IT" IN SCHOOL?

The homeschooling community is much more diverse than most people imagine. Yes, there are certainly people who choose homeschooling primarily for religious reasons, but families decide to leave traditional schools for a range of reasons. At most of the Liberated Learner centers you'll find a pretty common set of reasons why people decide to leave and choose a different path for their children:

- Kids who are bright but bored in school
- Kids who don't like the social atmosphere in school or are being bullied
- Kids who have learning differences that schools have a hard time addressing or won't address.

- Kids with strong passions who can't pursue them because of the time school consumes, such as dance or acting
- Kids who don't want three to four hours of homework a night (along with the stress, anxiety, and arguing with parents that this brings)
- Kids with chronic medical conditions that make it hard to attend school and who need more flexibility in scheduling
- Kids who would rather be tromping through the woods or building computers than sitting still and listening for seven hours a day

Ultimately, homeschooling is simply the legal mechanism that allows families to take control of the why, how, what, when, and where of learning and living. It provides the freedom and flexibility families and young people need to create the kind of life they want based on their particular situations and interests.

WHAT OPTIONS ARE THERE FOR KIDS WHO DON'T HAVE A SELF-DIRECTED LEARNING CENTER IN THEIR COMMUNITY?

Chances are that you do not live near a self-directed learning center. If a young person is struggling in school and would like to stop going in order to direct their own education, what options do they have? First and foremost, you can just stop going and register as a homeschooler. This option is legal in all fifty states and is very easy to do, despite the imposing-sounding text written into many homeschooling statutes. This is what most people who stop going to school do; they live independently as a homeschooler.

Despite not having the support of a self-directed learning center, you can create an incredibly rich and satisfying life and education by creating your own homeschooling program. If you have an Internet connection, you have access to any kind of knowledge and information that you could ever want. You can join organized online classes, you can learn about any topic you might have an interest in, you can connect to experts in various fields, and you can plan and arrange travel. The possibilities are endless.

Many families new to homeschooling worry about social and athletic aspects. There is likely a homeschooling community in your area that you can connect with that organizes educational and social outings. Depending on your state laws, homeschoolers are often allowed to participate in after-school activities and sports. If not, community based theater and sports leagues are a good option.

Young people can also utilize community members as mentors or teachers, perhaps trading work for lessons or other resources. There is an extensive literature on how to do independent homeschooling well, so I won't attempt to replicate it here. Just know that if school is not working for you, you can leave right now and begin creating your own path whether there is a self-directed learning center near you or not.

HOW DOES THIS APPLY TO YOUNGER CHILDREN?

Philosophically, the idea of child-centered, noncoercive education applies equally well, if not better, to younger children. If you've spent time around children, you've noticed that they are unbelievably curious about the world and ask a million questions. There is a lot of talk about teaching people how to learn, but all of the genetic hardware is already in place. Humans are learning creatures. We learn to walk and talk, pick up on social cues, and in the case of my three-year-old, unlock and navigate my iPhone without formal lessons. Kids learn by imitating, experimenting, playing, and trial and error. They know how to learn, and they do it well. We don't need to force them or provide rewards and punishments. The learning is reward enough.

Practically, programs need to be structured differently when working with younger children. Teens are welcome to come and go from our centers throughout the day without signing in or out. Obviously, you would not want seven-year-olds wandering out of the building without anyone knowing. You may need to have a higher staff-to-member ratio because younger kids might need more attention, as they are generally less self-sufficient. In New Jersey, at least, when you are working with younger children there is another and more extensive set of regulations concerning the building and your operations for child protection reasons. There are programs inside and outside of Liberated Learners that successfully use self-directed learning with younger children.

LIBERATED LEARNERS MEMBER PROFILE

Paul Scutt, Princeton/Bucks Learning Cooperatives

I got into education in a round-about way. I wanted to do something we called Youth Work in England, which was basically a social worker who would work with young people in schools. We would do a little teaching and also run clubs, and then we would spend half our time doing casework with families. Then Prime Minister Mrs. Thatcher came along and cut the funding for that type of work, so I went in for teaching full-time, got a degree in computer science, spent some time in the British Civil Service as a computer specialist, and then eventually became a teacher full-time.

I worked initially at an all-girls school in the Lake District in northern England because the job was available and because I am an avid outdoorsman and rock climber and this gave me many opportunities to be outside climbing. I was teaching math and introducing computers to the school as an after-school club. I eventually moved my family to Tanzania, where I had grown up, to work in international schools. I put up with the traditional teaching daytime stuff, but most of my enjoyment came from after-school activities in Africa with the Sailing Club—we were right next to the ocean—and we went up to Mt. Kilimanjaro and did some mountaineering twice a year. There was lots of stuff to do apart from sitting down and lecturing kids. I was teaching computer science, but it was very much not lecturing. It was showing people how to do things and then giving them the space to be creative and write programs. One of the programs I taught was the International Baccalaureate Math with Computing class, so there was a quite a bit of math involved.

I eventually made my way to the United States and worked at the United Nations School in New York teaching computers and math. I ended up working at a private school in Pennsylvania teaching mostly math and leading the rock-climbing club before leaving to help found Princeton Learning Cooperative. The private school had a reputation of being pretty free and open, and they didn't stipulate what teachers had to do as much as others schools do, so I was able to take my classes out into the fields and the forests and the woods during class time, and we would talk about math a little bit. At least a few of us had to carry textbooks around with us so that if the other teachers saw us they would see that we were doing something. That was fine. I enjoyed that. And then we did some great outdoor activities. Not just climbing but other stuff, too, so I got involved in that a little.

In 2006, Ken Robinson came out with his TED talk about schools killing creativity in kids. In my head, that idea had always been buzzing around. One of my teacher colleagues was a psychologist as well, so we were always chatting about what we could do to undermine the system. Basically, it was that Ken Robinson talk that undermined my confidence in what I was doing. I think the fact that we weren't allowing kids to be creative started to bother me. We weren't creating new knowledge. In England, they stress that to get an ordinary degree, you've got to write a proposal that is new knowledge. The idea is to be creative, to create new knowledge for the human race. That's how you get your degree. I always thought that there's no point to studying stuff that somebody has already done. That's useful as a tool, maybe, but the idea is to try to be creative and curious and do something with knowledge.

My life and work are significantly different working at PLC and BLC as opposed to traditional schools. One of the things that I really understand about humanity is the importance of relation-ships, and this is critical to what we do at PLC and BLC. We talk about being a mentor, which is almost like having your teen men-tees as family members. You really get to know them and try and be there for them. It's the most important thing we do and what I appreciate most about the work. I also like that at PLC and BLC we appreciate individuality. We allow kids to do whatever makes them feel comfortable and allow them to be themselves, which I think is very important.

10

have included the following collection of previous writings and speeches because they touch on some of the themes of this book and can stand alone in explaining what we do and why. Feel free to reproduce and distribute any of these as needed.

TWENTY-FIRST CENTURY LEARNING
Guest editorial for the Bucks County Courier Times, August 28, 2011

If you were to ask people to close their eyes and imagine the best way for young people to learn, how many would imagine an arrangement that looks or feels much like our current system of education? The idea that schools in the United States are in need of reform has widespread support. But the vast majority of proposals for how to do this tend to accept the basic structure of traditional schools. For the most part, minor fixes are proposed for major problems. Many people think if we just do *school* better, we will have a first-class educational system: make the days a bit longer, extend the school year, hire better teachers, give parents more choices through vouchers and charter schools, offer more extracurricular activities, limit class sizes. These ideas all have their place, and they are the types of fixes that may work for some kids and some schools. But I think they fall far short of creating the engaging learning environments that many children need.

Throughout my eleven years as a teacher I taught a wide range of students, the majority of whom were fine in school. But I also worked with a large number of students who had simply checked out or who were uninspired or bored.

They came to school almost every day, but they were only going through the motions, simply jumping through whatever hoops the school put in front of them and trying to get by with the least amount of effort. For them, high school felt less like an opportunity and more like a four-year prison sentence. These students could have gone to a private school or a charter school, and maybe it would have been a little smaller, a little nicer, a little better. But the fact remains that it would still be *school*.

In July, I attended a conference of people who are serious about offering another vision of what learning can be. It was hosted by North Star, a learning center in Hadley, Massachusetts. For the past fifteen years, North Star has taken advantage of the freedom and flexibility that homeschooling laws offer to help students leave school and develop a totally personalized education based on their passions and interests while avoiding the least desirable aspects of traditional schooling that have little or nothing to do with actual learning: standardized testing and prep, rigid scheduling, myriad rules and regulations, inflexible curriculum.

North Star helps families develop an educational plan and then offers the classes, tutoring, mentoring, and other services to make that plan a reality. North Star also gives students a hand with college counseling and helps in finding internship, travel, service, and employment opportunities—all in a safe and comfortable space where kids can work and socialize. Through this structure, North Star's staff is able to focus solely on what makes for a good education—a motivated student following his or her interests, knowledgeable adults who are willing to share their time and talents, and the freedom, support, and flexibility to accommodate all types of learners.

For a student who feels trapped and limited in school, this approach to learning can be a life-changing experience. In fact, it can be life changing for teachers, too. I have been so inspired by the example of North Star that I have decided to leave teaching this summer and help establish the Princeton Learning Cooperative, which will open this fall. While this type of education is not for every student, I believe there are millions of kids across the country who would benefit immediately and directly if an option like North Star or the Princeton Learning Cooperative existed in their community.

There are many talented and dedicated professionals working in traditional schools, and I've been happy to count myself among them. But in my opinion, the skills and abilities so crucial to the future success of our children—self-direction, creativity, the ability to collaborate, and flexibility—will not always be nurtured by traditionally structured schools. More often, they will be found in places like North Star and the Princeton Learning Cooperative.

DO YOU KNOW ANY TEENS WHO DON'T LIKE SCHOOL?

Guest editorial for Times of Trenton, December 16, 2014

As part of my job, I talk to a lot of people—folks at farmers markets and community festivals, and even strangers on the street—and I usually start the conversation by asking, "Know any teens who don't like school?" People usually laugh. I can only assume that's because teens not liking school is right up there with death and taxes.

Also predictable are the responses parents give when their children tell them that they don't like school: "You have to go to school. Even if you don't like it, it is good for you in the long run. How else do you expect to get into college, get a good job, and be able to support yourself and your family? People who don't go to school flip burgers, get addicted to drugs, and end up in the gutter."

The conventional wisdom holds that school is necessary to learn and to lead a fulfilling and successful life. Many kids, after all, find traditional school to be satisfying and useful—I certainly did—but many others do not.

But what if the conventional wisdom is wrong?

I ask the people I meet to consider a different life for teens. What if teens could still learn and make a life for themselves even if they didn't go to school? What if they could spend most of their time and energy doing what they love instead of being forced to focus on what they do not like or what they are not good at? What if they had zero busy work and instead filled their days with activities they find meaningful?

When I tell people this, they're generally interested but maybe a bit skeptical. So I'll continue: What if young people could set up internships and volunteer opportunities with experts in the local community to learn what various careers are really like before they spend tens of thousands of dollars switching their major five times in college? How about kids deciding to take a break and go for a walk on a beautiful day without being tracked down for truancy, or traveling for a life-changing experience (or a routine family vacation) and not returning to a mountain of missed assignments?

I tell parents that their kids can do all of this while being part of a caring community of other teens and adults who mentor them on this more independent path. That they could use the time otherwise spent on homework to write a novel, record an album, build their own computer, design a videogame, or tackle any other project they felt passionate about. That they can start college earlier by taking classes at the community colleges at sixteen or seventeen if they so choose, or they could take free online classes offered by some of the best colleges in the country.

The good news is that all of this can be reality and is possible right now—today—if a teen wants it. Teenagers can leave school legally and make the kind of life they want for themselves. And there are organizations all over the country that are reimagining how education can work for our young people and providing them with the freedom, flexibility, and support to leave school and find the right path for themselves and their families.

The simple truth is that the traditional educational system is no longer the only way. To learn more about how to turn frustrated teens into excited young men and women, do a Google search for my colleague Kenneth Danford's TEDx talk at Amherst College or take a look at Ken Robinson's talk on schools and creativity. I promise you'll be amazed at the opportunities present for teenagers who just do not like school.

LEARNING VS. SCHOOLING

Guest editorial for local newspaper

The most important lesson I learned during my eleven-year teaching career is that learning and schooling are not the same thing. Learning can certainly take place in schools, but what really changed my view of education, and ultimately my career, were the numerous cases I saw year after year where the structure of school actually prevented students from learning.

As a first-day-of-school exercise, I used to have my students write down what came to mind when they thought of the word *school*. A lot of the answers were obvious: books, paper, pencils, lunch, friends. But there was always a large group of kids who would reply with things like boring, prison, torture, and pointless. At first this puzzled me because I had always liked school and learning, and I knew that learning didn't feel pointless or torturous but rather exciting, liberating, and empowering. I see my young daughter learning new things all the time, bursting with enthusiasm. So how is it that we take these little learning machines we call children and thirteen years of schooling later we end up with a pretty big chunk of them totally disengaged and not wanting anything to do with learning? What would we think about libraries that made people not like books? Tennis camps that made people want to stop playing tennis?

Unfortunately, many people—parents, educators, politicians, and ultimately kids—have come to the conclusion that the only place to learn is in school. This simply is not true. Learning can happen all the time and in a variety of places. It does not have to look or feel anything like the traditional structure of school that turns off so many students to actual learning. The idea that the best way for children to learn is to pack each and every one of them into a building with a teacher, a textbook, and standardized tests seems more antiquated every day, especially when compared to the resources increasingly available to students and families outside of the traditional structure.

The Princeton Learning Cooperative, where I am a codirector, is one of these resources. We build a totally personalized curriculum and education based on the interests, abilities, and goals of our students. A good example of this process is Max. Max came to PLC after his eighth grade year. He is a bright kid but was totally disengaged in school. The program he has built over the past fourteen months with PLC's support was definitely the right move for him and his family. We took his interest in science and set up a one-on-one chemistry tutorial last year with supplemental video lessons online at Khan Academy. This year he is extending that interest by auditing the introductory chemistry class at Princeton University. He is learning computer programming by taking a class at PLC following the AP computer science curriculum.

Max loves the outdoors, and the flexibility of PLC's scheduling allows him to volunteer at Snipes Farm, where another PLC associate lives and has worked with Max on writing and early twentieth-century American literature. Max also learned rock climbing with my fellow PLC codirector, Paul Scutt (and learned so well that he was offered a part-time job by the climbing gym). As I write, Max and another of our students are sitting beside me, setting up a weekly book club. Max is taking calculus and biology and is participating in a graphic design class at PLC, in which he is currently learning how to use professional design software from an actual graphic designer. He goes to museums, rides his bike religiously, researches Russian history, will be working with a German major at Princeton University on introductory German. He has also learned to bake a mean apple pie.

The most important part about all of this is that every single activity I have listed, Max is doing voluntarily. At PLC we offer opportunities, but there are no requirements. Personally, it has been amazing to me as an educator to watch Max's inherent desire to learn reassert itself after being dampened by the structure of school. If you compare where Max would have been if he had stayed in school versus where he is now, it is no contest. Learning works for Max; schooling did not.

CREATING CHANGE IN FARMING AND EDUCATION
Guest editorial on BucksHappeningmag.com, September2014

Princeton Learning Cooperative and Snipes Farm and Education Center in Pennsylvania recently announced a partnership, arousing some curiosity in Mercer County. After all, what do education and farming have in common?

Traditionally, the answer is very little except for the occasional school trip to a farm. This new partnership, however, represents something quite different because both of our organizations are deeply committed to creating fundamental change in our industries. A partnership, therefore, makes eminent sense. Let me explain.

Through sophisticated technologies, the use of bio-engineered seeds and massive amounts of chemical fertilizers, pesticides, and herbicides, modern industrial farms today are able to produce fields of perfectly aligned rows of corn for as far as the eye can see. From a certain standpoint this is a beautiful and wonderful thing to behold until we consider that to achieve this "perfection," industrial farming imposes enormous costs through loss of biodiversity, pollution from chemical runoff, and in the case of animal production, a tremendous amount of suffering.

In the modern farm, very little thought is given to what is actually good for the local environment and the people, plants, and animals that depend on it for life. The goal is a highly standardized "one-size-fits-all" product.

In much the same way, modern education is also pushing for increased standardization and testing to ensure a "uniform product." Think of hundreds or thousands of kids sitting in perfectly aligned desks, in required classes, using a curriculum based on common core standards and preparing for standardized state tests.

Once again, from a certain view, this looks good and produces high school graduates who are considered "proficient," but few people think about the costs associated with this "one-size-fits-all" approach to learning.

During my teaching career, I saw these costs firsthand: kids who were bright but bored to tears; students who were bullied for being different; kids who had learning differences that couldn't be addressed in the traditional system; kids who would rather be out exploring in the woods than sitting still and listening for seven hours a day; kids who had real passions and talents that were pushed to the side by three to four hours of homework a night; and families that endured so much stress from the nightly battles over doing that homework.

There is a growing awareness of the costs associated with modern farming practices. Snipes Farm and Education Center is part of the movement to show that local, organic, and sustainable agriculture can produce food in a way that protects and nourishes everything that it touches—the soil, the plants and animals, the water, the farmers, and ultimately us, the people who eat it.

There is also a national movement that recognizes the heavy costs of the one-size-fits-all approach to education and wants to replace it with learning opportunities that light a fire within children, as opposed to smothering them with tests. Princeton Learning Cooperative is helping to lead this movement and is spreading the knowledge that families can in fact opt out of this standardized system and create a life and education for their children that will work for them, one that is based on their interests and talents.

We don't need perfect rows of corn or children at desks. We need a food and education system that recognizes the inherent value of our land and our children and works to nourish both.

OPTING OUT IN A BIGGER WAY

Guest editorial in Times of Trenton, May 1, 2015

Schools throughout New Jersey are gearing up to give another round of PARCC standardized testing. Families are rightly opting out of these tests. Tests measure a very narrow range of skills and abilities. They can't possibly measure what we value most in young people: creativity, inspiration, kindness, curiosity, and collaboration. In fact, the focus on standards and testing can actually undermine these things. Tests and test prep can squeeze out of schools the most important parts of education.

Some parents, however, feel that the problem goes deeper than just the tests. One way to look at the PARCC and other standardized tests is that they are just the most visible and controversial part of the traditional public and private school system that has increasingly moved away from focusing on the needs and interests of young people and relies more and more on state standards and rigid requirements.

Some parents have come to feel that the entire system and philosophy of traditional schooling is not a good fit for their children. They know that learning should not be based on a set of state or district standards but rather on the interests, abilities, and goals of children and their families.

Because of this, some families are opting out of the school system in a bigger way.

What does this entail? The most widely recognized and efficient way to opt out of the school system in the United States is called homeschooling. Although the name brings to mind images of doing school at home with parents as teachers, homeschooling can involve a wide array of learning opportunities and channels. Homeschooling is simply the legal mechanism—like the opt-out forms for the tests—that gives families the freedom and flexibility to create the kind of life and education that works best for their children.

The main advantage of homeschooling is that the family has full control over what, when, and how learning happens. Take, for example, a middle schooler who has a serious interest in computers, programming, and gaming. I know from firsthand experience that it is very hard for a school to feed an interest like this in any serious way. There might be some computer use in various classes. Maybe there is a computer elective that meets every other day or once a week for forty-five minutes. Maybe there is an after-school club of some kind. All of these are fringe activities. The main experiences of this computer-minded middle schooler would be activities that are irrelevant to his or her big interests. Add in hours of homework a night, leaving only scraps of time and energy to pursue his or her passions, and this child may find his or her life deeply frustrating.

What if this young person's family opted him or her out of the traditional school system? Instead of computers being a peripheral part of this child's education, they could be the central focus and the anchor for all sorts of other kinds of learning. Once you step out of the traditional system, there are so many amazing resources available to families. A child passionate about computers may learn programming on sites like Code Academy, explore work and career options with a local programmer, and design and build his or her own computers. The child could volunteer or intern at a local computer repair store or software company, use free online software to start designing and building his or her own games, or get involved at the NYU Game Center, which holds a variety of public events.

All of a sudden this child—who may have viewed school as boring or just something to get through—is excited about life and learning again. The child is engaged in the things that speak most to him or her and sees a direct connection with what he or she wants in life and the way he or she spends the majority of time.

That's what opting out can look like.

I work at Princeton Learning Cooperative. We support families and teens to opt out of school to create the kind of life they want for themselves. We mostly work with families coming from traditional public and private schools, families who had never considered homeschooling as an option before. We offer various supports to make opting out of school a practical reality: a small and caring community of adults and other teens, classes, tutoring, mentoring, trips, help finding intern and volunteer opportunities, and help with college admissions.

If your dissatisfaction with standardized education goes beyond just the tests and you are interested in exploring opting out in a bigger way—either as an independent homeschooling family or as a Princeton Learning Cooperative family—we're happy to help you get started, whatever the right path is for you.

Interested in finding out more? You can find a wealth of resources at the New Jersey Homeschool Association at http://jerseyhomeschool.net/. And to learn more about PLC, you can visit our website: http://princetonlearningco-operative.org.

THE WHY, HOW, AND WHAT OF PLC

Speech at 2015 PLC Celebration of Self-Directed Learning

Most of the time when I talk with families interested in PLC or volunteers, teens, or community members, I end up talking a lot about *what* we do and *how* we do it, but very rarely do we chat about *why* PLC exists. I'd like to take a brief moment to talk about this before we get to our speakers for today.

What we do is pretty straight forward: we are a center that offers academic and nonacademic support for teenagers four days a week. This includes classes, tutoring, mentoring, help finding work and volunteer opportunities, trips, college admissions help, and a safe and welcoming community for teens. That's pretty simple, and there are a lot of other people and organizations that offer these kinds of things.

How we do what we do is a bit more interesting. And it starts with this little nugget: we offer a way for teenagers to leave school permanently ... and use homeschooling law to create a personalized education based on what they are interested in. By homeschooling, we don't mean replicating school at home or parents teaching their kids, just the legal mechanism to unenroll or opt out of school so that you can create the kind of life and education you want.

And everything we offer is voluntary. We don't require or make kids do anything. There are no attendance requirements, grades, credits, or diplomas because we are not a school. We offer opportunities, resources, and support, but we don't mandate participation or coerce young people to do any particular thing.

But I think *why* we do this makes us special and is the reason our little tribe of members and supporters dedicate so much of their time and effort to the Princeton Learning Cooperative.

Because if you walk through any school today, you will find a group of kids who thrive in that environment and love it, but you will also find a large number of kids who go through the motions, jump through hoops, bide their time, not feeling any kind of purpose or excitement in what they do.

School is just something to get through. It doesn't provide any kind of spark. And you will also find a group of kids who find school intolerable and feel stuck, and the whole experience makes them miserable.

It's just like the world of work for adults. How many people do you know who just punch the clock, drag themselves to work every day just for the paycheck, and don't feel any sort of meaning or purpose to how they spend a majority of their waking hours?

This situation pains us, not only for the adults, but especially for the young people. We want people to feel that life is good, life is worth living to the fullest, and there isn't a lot of time, so we shouldn't waste it being stuck in situations that make us miserable. We want to empower people to take control of their lives and work to make the kind of life they want for themselves.

And so PLC exists to profoundly improve the daily lives of teens and their families, not in some sort of theoretical or abstract way, but right now, today. We believe people thrive when they have control over their lives and time, have positive relationships with the people around them, and are doing what they consider to be meaningful work.

This is the kind of life we want teens to have right now, not four or five or six years down the road, and this is why we pour so much of our time, love, and effort into PLC.

WELL-BEING

Opening Remarks at a Teen Wellness Panel Discussion in Princeton, 2014

I went into my teaching career with a huge amount of enthusiasm and idealism about changing the world through education. I was going to be the beacon, the guiding light for my students as we marched our way up the mountain of knowledge to the summit of wisdom, or some such thing, and it was going to be wonderful and enriching and enlightening for everyone, especially the students.

Certainly some of the young people I taught during those years felt that way about what we were doing, but a big chunk of them felt more like this:

- Is this going to be on the test?
- Do we *have* to do that?
- How wide can the margins be?
- Is there extra credit?
- And so on.

School was just not doing it for them. Not to mention the kids who actively rebelled against what they were being asked to do. And it made me start to think about why some kids thrive in the traditional system and why some don't.

In my career I came across a lot of kids who were brilliant but had a 2 percent in my class because they refused to do anything for it. I had kids who refused to come to school at all. Kids that no matter how simplified you made it and how often you went over it just didn't "get it."

It made me take a step back and think in more general terms: What do kids need in their lives to thrive and have well-being, recognizing that school or whatever educational institution they are at plays a huge role in their lives?

I think the types of things that lead to a sense of well-being for teens are not very different from the types of things that lead to well-being for adults. In my mind, these are the big ones:

- **Meaningful work**—you like what you do on a daily basis, and what you do seems to have a purpose and is useful.

- **Positive and healthy relationships**—this can be parents, adult mentors, role models, friends, and other teens.
- **Ongoing, increasing autonomy**—you have a large say in how you spend your time (this is particularly big for teens as they are transitioning into adult life).
- **Safe and supportive community**—it's really hard to focus or think about anything else if you are constantly worried about something bad happening to you at any given moment.

So it seems like these are some of the big things—meaningful work, good relationships, autonomy, and a supportive community you can call home.

The question tonight is how can we help teens have these things. What types of structures or school environments can we provide that can promote these things and lead to well-being for teens?

I think the answer is that, just as there is a wide diversity of people, there should be a wide diversity of educational settings. I think it is really difficult to craft one system that works for everyone.

Some young people can get what they need in the traditional school system. I certainly did. I attended public high school in Ohio, and I never felt limited in any way. I generally liked it. I had a group of friends and good teachers that I liked. It was safe. There weren't draconian rules and regulations, and I liked the things I was involved in like sports, the school newspaper, and French club, etc.

But what I learned from my teaching career in public schools in Pennsylvania, however, was that not everyone has an experience like that. I taught a segment of teens who found the work dull or pointless, who didn't connect with their peers or the staff, who were bullied, who felt that there were too many rules and regulations, who didn't feel safe, and who dreaded going to school—public or private.

Our mission when we started PLC was to help teens leave traditional public and private schools and create lives and educations based on their interests, goals, and abilities and to be very direct about trying to give teens the opportunity to have what they need to thrive.

We didn't want to start another school, whether it was a progressive private school or a charter school. It might have been smaller or nicer, but essentially it would have still been school. And there would still be red tape in the sense that you have regulations, whether from the state or accrediting institutions, that would impact how we would work with our members.

We decided that the most direct and simple way to get what we wanted was to have the teens we work with register as homeschoolers, not in the sense of their parents teaching them at home or replicating school at home or PLC, but simply as the legal mechanism to withdraw from the traditional system. Then you have all the freedom and flexibility you could ever want to create the kind of life and education that will work for you.

We also decided that everything we would offer would be voluntary. One of the reasons that I left teaching was that essentially I felt like my life consisted of making kids who didn't want to be there do things they didn't want to do. It was not a pleasant way to go through life. I wanted to work with kids to help them get better at the things they loved and wanted to do.

Now I'll just talk briefly about how these big things that feed into teen well-being are addressed at PLC.

- **Autonomy:** As I said, everything that happens at PLC is voluntary, including attendance, participating in classes or tutorials, etc. Some people would say that is too much autonomy for teens to be making those kinds of decisions. We think that the most important way for people to get good at something is to practice. So taking real responsibility for your life and learning is the best way to become a responsible adult, which doesn't mean teens don't make mistakes and bad decisions, just like adults. Each of our members has a staff mentor that he or she meets with individually each week to help him or her think about decisions and reflect about what has happened and how to maybe adjust things in the future.
- **Meaningful work:** PLC is not a school in the sense that we have a course catalog with classes to choose from or required classes that you must take. We start with the interests of the teen and go from there.

So if someone joins and wants to learn conversational Russian, none of our staff know that, so we go out through our contacts and try to find volunteers or university work-study students to work with our member. If we can't find someone, we help teens find other ways and other resources to learn what they want through online, volunteer, or other resources. So ideally, the students are engaged in learning and activities both at PLC and outside of PLC that they find meaningful and useful.

- **Positive relationships:** What seems absolutely critical during adolescence are the social aspects of their lives. Our common room is usually packed with kids hanging out, chatting, playing ping-pong, and watching YouTube videos together. And what seems like wasting time—why aren't they studying?—is actually extremely valuable, as they are learning how to make connections and navigate the social world.

- **Safe and welcoming community:** We try really hard to make PLC a safe and welcoming community. We have all-group meetings once a week in which we discuss issues that come up at PLC and make decisions about group trips and classes together. We are intentionally a small community so that everyone knows each other and can hopefully relate to each other in a personal manner.

This kind of learning is obviously not for everyone. It is sort of like the difference between working a corporate job where your tasks are given to you by someone higher up the chain versus owning your own small business where the decisions are your own to a large extent.

What we have found in our four years of existence is that if you give teenagers the time and space to figure out what they want in life and the support to pursue it willingly and enthusiastically, this kind of environment can be life changing.

WHEN HELPING ISN'T HELPFUL

Unpublished essay

I've learned a lot from my four-year-old daughter: who Dora, Boots, and Swiper are; how to turn our couch cushions into an airport; and how to play grumpy old troll at the playground. One of the more profound lessons she has taught me is to redefine the concept of "help." I'm still struggling with this one, and many PLC parents we talk with struggle with this as well.

I consider myself to be an organized, goal-oriented, and efficient person. I get things done with a minimal amount of messing around or wasted time. My daughter, on the other hand, is not. She's four. Everything takes ten times longer when she does it as opposed to when I do it for her—brushing her teeth, putting on her shoes, getting dressed, buckling herself into her booster seat, etc. Instead of me buckling her into her seat in about two seconds, she turns it into, in some cases, a ten-minute battle of wills if I leave her to her own devices. Sometimes watching her cut up her own noodles for minutes on end while spilling them all over the place is agonizing and excruciating for me to watch. Wouldn't it be so much simpler and efficient for me to just pick up the fork and do it for her? No mess and we get to eat sooner. Mission accomplished. Sure, she has cut up paper and left it all over the floor, but wouldn't it just be easier for me to clean it up and avoid the inevitable fussing and foot-dragging that asking her to clean it up would entail?

What I have come to realize, however, is that when I take over and do things for her that she can or should be doing for herself, I am not helping her; I'm helping myself by making my life easier and robbing her of opportunities to learn and grow and take more responsibility for herself.

I'm still struggling with this at home and also at PLC. Some of the hardest, best work I do at PLC is to just sit on my hands and wait for the kids to figure it out themselves. For example, I'm sitting in the common room listening to a group of kids try to organize rides to an ice-skating outing on a Friday. This is simple, right? Who is driving? How many people can they each take? How many people are going? Assign people to the cars and we're ready to go. Maybe two minutes, tops. Except it's not easy. The kids haven't had the chance and opportunity to really be in charge of organizing something like this before, and it's all getting screwed up. People are getting left behind, no one knows whose car they are in, do they need another driver? Every bone in my body is aching to grab a piece of paper and start organizing this thing the right way.

But no. Stepping in and organizing the trip would only be helping me out and robbing the kids of the opportunity to learn how to organize a trip.

I can't say that the trip went off without a hitch, but by allowing the kids to take responsibility for it and learn from their mistakes, they took one more step toward self-direction and autonomy. This same process plays out all the time in the way kids choose to spend their time at PLC, what they choose to study or not study, and the bigger choices they make about their lives. It is very rarely efficient, mistake-free, or without ups and downs, but we feel that the benefits of this approach to education and living are worth the trouble in the end.

There are obvious ways for adults to be helpful to teenagers (drive to the ice-skating rink, help kids reflect when things don't go well, listen to their concerns and offer advice if asked), but sometimes the way to be truly helpful is to step back and just support them in taking more responsibility for their lives.

Appendix: Additional Resources

1. PLC FINANCIALS
1.1. Year 1 PLC Financials

Princeton Learning Cooperative's first year financials are included to provide context about the items that are typically in a budget and also the relative amounts for each item. During our first year, we had one staff member, rented a single room in downtown Princeton and ended the year with seven members. Other Liberated Learners centers have worked with more teens and had larger budgets during their first year so PLC's finances represent a small and slow startup.

	Jul '10 - Jun 11
Ordinary Income/Expense	
Income	
43000 · Donations	
43200 · Restricted Donations	3,993.98
43400 · Unrestrictred Donations	8,865.68
Total 43000 · Donations	12,859.66
47200 · Program Income	
47230 · Net Tuition	
47231 · Gross Tuition	30,400.00
Total 47230 · Net Tuition	30,400.00
Total 47200 · Program Income	30,400.00
Total Income	43,259.66

Expense

60800 · Fundraising Expenses	375.00
60900 · Business Expenses	
60920 · Business Registration Fees	920.00
Total 60900 · Business Expenses	920.00
62100 · Contract Services	
62140 · Legal Fees	1,867.92
Total 62100 · Contract Services	1,867.92
62800 · Facilities and Equipment	
62890 · Rent, Parking, Utilities	9,465.00
Total 62800 · Facilities and Equipment	9,465.00
65000 · Operations	
65004 · Advertising	429.02
65008 · Website	326.91
65010 · Books, Subscriptions, Reference	159.53
65020 · Postage, Mailing Service	159.27
65030 · Printing and Copying	2,296.31
65040 · Supplies	946.26
Total 65000 · Operations	4,317.30
65100 · Other Types of Expenses	

65120 · Insurance - Liability, D and O	3,290.00
Total 65100 · Other Types of Expenses	3,290.00
66000 · Payroll Expenses	
66100 · Health Insurance Reimbursements	9,539.36
66200 · Payroll Services	1,101.95
66300 · Salary	8,059.11
66000 · Payroll Expenses - Other	594.86
Total 66000 · Payroll Expenses	19,295.28
68300 · Travel and Meetings	
68310 · Conference, Convention, Meeting	473.13
68320 · Travel	88.03
Total 68300 · Travel and Meetings	561.16
Total Expense	40,091.66
Net Ordinary Income	3,168.00
Net Income	3,168.00

1.2. Year 2 PLC Financials

Princeton Learning Cooperative's second year financials are included to show the growth of the program over two years. These financials represent finishing the year with 22 members, two full-time staff, and moving to a larger space midway through the year. Our budget after 6 years and including both Princeton and Bucks Learning Cooperatives calls for $340,000 in income and a total of $260,000 in payroll expenses for five full-time employees.

	Jul '11 - Jun 12
Ordinary Income/Expense	
Income	
43000 · Donations	
43200 · Restricted Donations	3,458.24
43400 · Unrestrictred Donations	28,089.50
Total 43000 · Donations	31,547.74
47200 · Program Income	
47210 · Consulting	2,200.00
47220 · Space Usage	0.00
47230 · Net Tuition	
47231 · Gross Tuition	84,800.00
Total 47230 · Net Tuition	84,800.00
Total 47200 · Program Income	87,000.00
Total Income	118,547.74
Expense	
60800 · Fundraising Expenses	727.79
60900 · Business Expenses	
60920 · Business Registration Fees	50.00
60900 · Business Expenses - Other	25.00
Total 60900 · Business Expenses	75.00
62100 · Contract Services	
62110 · Accounting Fees	3,200.00
62120 · Consulting	600.00
62150 · Work Study Students	0.00
62160 · Background Checks	19.95
Total 62100 · Contract Services	3,819.95
62800 · Facilities and Equipment	
62890 · Rent, Parking, Utilities	14,780.50
Total 62800 · Facilities and Equipment	14,780.50
65000 · Operations	
65004 · Advertising	1,261.83
65008 · Website	137.25
65010 · Books, Subscriptions, Reference	50.00
65020 · Postage, Mailing Service	128.08

65030 · Printing and Copying	532.83
65040 · Supplies	626.60
Total 65000 · Operations	2,736.59
65100 · Other Types of Expenses	
65120 · Insurance - Liability, D and O	3,788.37
Total 65100 · Other Types of Expenses	3,788.37
66000 · Payroll Expenses	
66100 · Health Insurance Reimbursements	10,618.08
66200 · Payroll Services	463.50
66300 · Salary	46,420.48
66400 · Payroll Taxes	5,515.24
66000 · Payroll Expenses - Other	0.00
Total 66000 · Payroll Expenses	63,017.30
68300 · Travel and Meetings	
68310 · Conference, Convention, Meeting	101.78
Total 68300 · Travel and Meetings	101.78
Total Expense	89,047.28
Net Ordinary Income	29,500.46
Net Income	29,500.46

2. HOMESCHOOLING RESEARCH

2.1 Introduction

The following is a selected list of research studies looking at homeschooling, self-directed learning, and its long-term impacts. Thank you to Alison Snieckus for compiling this list.

2.2. Surveys of Grown Unschoolers

Unschooling is a branch of homeschooling that advocates self-directed learning. Unschooling children and teens are encouraged to learn from direct life experiences, for example play, interactions with others of all ages, reading, investigating and pursuing interests, personal and family responsibilities, volunteer and work experience, travel, and self-chosen classes. Parents and other adults offer the freedom, flexibility, and support for a young person to do so.

Here are two surveys of adult unschoolers on their educational experiences and lives after:

Gray, P. & Riley. G (2015). "Grown Unschoolers' Evaluations of Their Unschooling Experiences: Report I on a Survey of 75 Unschooled Adults." *Other Education: The Journal of Educational Alternatives,* 4(2), pp. 8-32. http://www.othereducation.org/index.php/OE/article/view/104.

Riley, G., & Gray, P. (2015). Grown unschoolers' experiences with higher education and employment: Report II on a survey of 75 unschooled adults. *Other Education: The Journal of Educational Alternatives,* 4(2), pp. 33-53. http://www.othereducation.org/index.php/OE/article/view/105/0.

And here are three blog posts from Peter Gray's *Freedom to Learn* blog at psychologytoday.com summarizing the research findings from those surveys:

- "A Survey of Grown Unschoolers I: Overview of Findings," June 7, 2014, https://www.psychologytoday.com/blog/freedom-learn/201406/survey-grown-unschoolers-i-overview-findings.
- "Survey of Grown Unschoolers II: Going On to College," June 17, 2014, https://www.psychologytoday.com/blog/freedom-learn/201406/survey-grown-unschoolers-ii-going-college.
- "Survey of Grown Unschoolers III: Pursuing Careers," June 21, 2014, https://www.psychologytoday.com/blog/freedom-learn/201406/survey-grown-unschoolers-iii-pursuing-careers.

2.3. Studies of Homeschooling

There are a number of investigations into the outcomes of homeschooling that conclude that homeschoolers fare well academically, socially, and emotionally. Conclusions from these studies are limited, however, in that none can attribute cause and effect and definitively say that homeschooling was the reason for the outcome. An aspect of the family's situation or its parenting style may well have contributed most significantly to the outcome. The citations that follow are also discussed in the Gray and Riley studies listed above.

Cogan, M.F. (2010). Exploring academic outcomes of homeschooled students. *Journal of College Admissions*, 6, 19–24. (http://eric.ed.gov/?id=EJ893891)

Gloeckner, G. W., & Jones, P. (2013). Reflections on a decade of changes in homeschooling and the homeschooled into higher education. *Peabody Journal of Education*, 88, 309-323. (http://peabody.vanderbilt.edu/faculty/pje/pje_volume_88_issue_3_2013/gloeckner_jones.php)

Martin-Chang, S., Gould, O.N., & Meuse, R.E. (2011). The impact of schooling on academic achievement: Evidence from homeschooled and traditionally schooled students. *Canadian Journal of Behavioral Science*, 43, 195–202. (https://www.researchgate.net/publication/232544669_The_Impact_of_Schooling_on_Academic_Achievement_Evidence_From_Homeschooled_and_Traditionally_Schooled_Students)

Medlin, R. G. (2013). Homeschooling and the question of socialization revisited. *Peabody Journal of Education*, 88, 284–297. (http://peabody.vanderbilt.edu/faculty/pje/pje_volume_88_issue_3_2013/medlin.php)

Ray, B. D. (2013). Homeschooling associated with beneficial learner and societal outcomes but educators do not promote it. *Peabody Journal of Education*, 88, 324–341. (http://peabody.vanderbilt.edu/faculty/pje/pje_volume_88_issue_3_2013/ray.php)

3. SAMPLE COLLEGE ADMISSIONS PAPERWORK

The following is an actual narrative transcript used in a PLC member's successful college application to a respected public university in Ohio. As reflected in the transcript, he took some courses at a local private high school before going on homebound instruction for a brief time, then joining PLC and finally finishing his senior year at the local community college. This transcript is provided to show an example of how self-directed learning can be documented in a format that colleges understand and also to show how PLC can be used for only a portion of a teen's high school career.

3.1. Official Transcript Summary

Student Name: Ethan
Report Date: (withheld)
Address: (withheld)
Parent's Names: (withheld)
Phone No: (withheld)
Birthdate: (withheld)
School Name: (withheld)

Course	Provider	Credits
English 9 (9th)	Solebury School	1
English 10 (10th)	Solebury School/CRSD/PLC/Self-Study	1
English 11 (11th)	PLC/Self-Study	1
Composition 111 (12th)	Bucks County Community College	.5 (planned)

Composition 110 (12th)	Bucks County Community College	.5 (in progress)
Honors Geometry (9th)	Solebury School	1
Honors Algebra 2/Trigonometry (10th)	Solebury School/CRSD/PLC	1
Probability and Statistics (11th)	PLC/Self-Study	1
Math 125—Pre-Calculus (12th)	Bucks County Community College	.5 (in progress)
Math 140—Calculus 1 (12th)	Bucks County Community College	.5 (planned)

Conceptual Physics (9th)	Solebury School	1
Honors Chemistry (10th)	Solebury School/CRSD/PLC/Self-Study	1
Biology (11th)	PLC/Self-Study	1
SCIE 102—Astronomy (12th)	Bucks County Community College	.5 (planned)

World History 9 (9th)	Solebury School	1
Honors Ethics (10th)	Solebury School	0.33
US History (10th)	PLC/Self-Study	0.66
Material History (11th)	Self-Study	1
Geography (12th)	Self-Study	.5
Spanish 2 (9th)	Solebury School	1
Spanish 3 (10th)	Solebury School/CRSD/Private Tutor	1

Photography (9th)	Solebury School/Self-Study	0.5
Introductory Art (10th)	Solebury School/Self-Study	0.33
Cooking (11th)	PLC/Self-Study	0.5
Driver's Ed (11th)	Self-Study	0.25
Teach2Serve (Social Entrepreneurship) (10th)	Solebury School	0.33

Small Business (11th)	Self-Study	1
Health (9th)	Solebury School/Self-Study	0.25
Personal Fitness I (9th)	Solebury School/Self-Study	1
Personal Fitness II (11th)	Self-Study	1
Total Credits		22.25

3.2. Course Information

Ethan began his high school career at the Solebury School in New Hope, Pennsylvania, for ninth and most of tenth grade before withdrawing for medical reasons. He was briefly enrolled in the Council Rock School District (CRSD) for homebound instruction before choosing to homeschool. He enrolled at the Princeton Learning Cooperative (PLC) to support his home-schooling for the end of tenth grade and then for eleventh and twelfth grade. Ethan enrolled part-time in Bucks County Community College during his twelfth-grade year and continues to engage in self-study.

During Ethan's high school career, he took courses from the following institutions:

- Solebury School, New Hope, Pennsylvania—*an official transcript has been ordered, to be mailed directly from the high school.*
- Council Rock School District, Newtown, Pennsylvania—*Ethan was enrolled only briefly during his transition from Solebury, so there is no official transcript, but evaluations from his homebound instructors are included in the course descriptions below.*

- Bucks County Community College, Newtown, Pennsylvania—*an official transcript has been ordered, to be mailed directly from the college.*
- Princeton Learning Cooperative, Princeton, New Jersey—*PLC is a nonprofit learning center that works with teenagers to create their own educational plans based on their interests, goals, and abilities. PLC offers classes, tutoring, and other activities to support student learning. Classes meet weekly, usually for one hour unless otherwise arranged, and are based on ability and interest rather than age. Students are encouraged to extend their study of the topics outside of class. Classes are taught by PLC staff, community volunteers, and Princeton University students. No grades or credits are awarded.*

Grades are not provided on the summary transcript, as the varying providers use different grading systems. See transcripts from Solebury School and Bucks County Community College for further information. For convenience, credits listed on this summary transcript indicate a full year of study (1) or a fractional year of study (.5, .33, .25) and do not reflect the credits granted by the particular educational institutions that provided the courses of study.

The listing of courses below provides a description and learning narrative for self-study and Princeton Learning Cooperative courses.

English 10: (Solebury School/Council Rock/Princeton Learning Cooperative/ Self-Study)

Course Description: The first third of this class was taken at Solebury School. In this course, students read and examined world literature and became familiar with certain schools of literary criticism that are useful to an understanding and appreciation of this literature. Through novels, short stories, poetry, and oral tales, this class explored literature often overlooked because of nationality, ethnicity, race, or gender of the author. The following questions were examined: (1) Is it important to read mainly from the canon of "great books" from a particular region or from the canon of "great books" of the world?; (2) What are the expectations for reading in an academic setting, and why is this style of reading expected?; (3) What is to be gained from comparing various literary styles from around the world?; (4) How can we use our exposure to various literatures to develop our own writing style?; (5) When reading literature, is it important to pay attention to the historical context of each work?; (6) Is it important to be able to formally analyze literature, and what does formal analysis entail? This course included a mandatory summer reading assignment. The Council Rock portion of the class consisted of finishing work from Solebury and assorted other topics (see evaluation below from the Council Rock teacher). The last portion of this class was completed as a self-study and consisted of reading a number of books on my own.

Texts: The following texts were used for the course:

- *The Color Purple* by Alice Walker
- *Othello* by William Shakespeare
- *Things Fall Apart* by Chinua Achebe
- *The Wave* by Todd Strasser
- *The Red Pyramid* by Rick Riordan
- *The Throne of Fire* by Rick Riordan
- *The Serpent's Shadow* by Rick Riordan
- *Maus I* and *Maus II* by Art Spiegelman
- The Oedipus Cycle (*Oedipus Rex, Oedipus at Colonus, Antigone*) by Sophocles (Trans. Dudley Fitts and Robert Fitzgerald)
- *Siddhartha* by Hermann Hesse

Evaluation: Solebury School provided trimester grades for the portion of the class taken at Solebury. Council Rock homebound instructor provided the following feedback for Ethan's English 10 work:

During Ethan's homebound instruction, he worked on many areas of a standard tenth grade curriculum. He finished reading *The Color Purple*, had discussions on the conflicts, characters and changes in the story, wrote an essay on life hardships and completed a theme analysis paper for the novel. For all of the assignments relating to *The*

Color Purple, Ethan went above and beyond in his dedication. His work ethic showed, as he received As on each of the papers and was very knowledgeable in his discussion of the story. Every other week Ethan was asked to learn twenty vocabulary words and was quizzed at random. Though the words came from a packet provided by The Solebury School, they were similar to words he'd see in *Sadlier-Oxford Vocabulary* books (Level E or F). Ethan was also given grammar work on a weekly basis. The depth of the work was fairly extensive. I would introduce a grammar rule, we would work together on examples and then Ethan needed to complete exercises on his own. He was quizzed on grammar approximately every two weeks. In my time with him, all of his grammar work was an A- or higher. Toward the end of our time together, Ethan and I were reading *Othello*. I think that it's important to read a play aloud to fully understand the plot points and drama. We read together and discussed the reading, and Ethan also responded to thematic prompts in writing. As always, he did incredibly well. Ethan should have no trouble adjusting to a new school environment (even if it's from home) because he is a conscientious student who truly cares about his future.

English 11: (Princeton Learning Cooperative/Self-Study)
Course Description: This course consisted of a number of language-based activities. I participated in the Writing for Life class at the Princeton Learning Cooperative that met once a week and included time and support in a number of different genres of writing, including e-mail, resumes, short stories, essay writing, and creative writing. I attended a nineteen-week-long SAT prep class that focused on composition and practice on SAT essay writing. I independently read a number of books, listed below.

Texts:

- *Lord of the Flies* by William Golding
- *Of Mice and Men* by John Steinbeck

- *A Wrinkle in Time* by Madeleine L'Engle
- *Every Day* by David Levithan
- *The Card Turner* by Louis Sachar
- *Things Not Seen* by Andrew Clements
- *Chance* by Amir Aczel
- *Knightly and Son* by Rohan Gavin
- *Stupid Fast* by Geoff Herbach
- *Mr. Penumbra's 24 Hour Book Store* by Robin Sloan

Honors Algebra II/Trigonometry: (Solebury School/Council Rock/ Princeton Learning Cooperative)

Course Description: The first third of this class was taken at Solebury School. The course was a faster paced and more in-depth analysis of the topics covered in Algebra II and Trigonometry, recommended for students who plan to go on in mathematics, science, or a related field. The subject matter included a brief review of first-degree polynomials followed by an in-depth study of higher-power polynomials, conic sections, and exponential, logarithmic, and trigonometric functions. Attention was given to the relationship between functions and their graphs. The Council Rock portion of the class consisted of continuing with a variety of mathematical concepts begun at Solebury (see evaluation below). The final portion of this class was taken at the Princeton Learning Cooperative. I worked with PLC staff member Justin to finish the material from the course relating to trigonometry.

Text: *Algebra 2* by Prentice Hall

Evaluation: Solebury School provided trimester grades for the portion of the class taken at Solebury. The Council Rock homebound instructor gave the following feedback:

Topic	Grade for homework	Grade for test
Functions and inverses	14/14	None given
Operations with roots and exponents	24/28	53/55
Use of imaginary numbers	5/5	None given
Exponential and logarithmic functions	30/30	78/100
Operations with rational functions and variations	Homework not turned in homebound instruction discontinued	Not able to administer
	Summary of grades	206/230 = 89.565%

Probability and Statistics: (PLC/Self-study)

Course Description: This course introduced students to the major concepts, logic, and issues in statistical reasoning and the tools involved in collecting, analyzing, and drawing conclusions from data. Four broad conceptual themes were explored:

- Exploring data: observing patterns and departures from patterns
- Planning a study: deciding what and how to measure
- Anticipating patterns: producing models using probability and simulation
- Statistical inference: confirming models

Text and Components: The main content of the course was delivered online via the Open Learning Initiatives (OLI) Probability & Statistics course (created by Carnegie Mellon University): www.oli.cmu.edu. The course included many "Learn by Doing" exercises, which I completed using Microsoft Excel. I participated in a weekly Statistics class at PLC in which students reviewed concepts learned online and engaged in hands-on group projects, many of which used spreadsheets and statistical software to analyze data. I did a final project analyzing data from NHL playoffs over a six-year period.

Honors Chemistry: (Solebury School/Council Rock/Princeton Learning Cooperative/Self-Study)
Course Description: The first third of this class was taken at Solebury School. This is the honors version of Chemistry and is designed for students who have an interest in exploring chemistry in more detail than the regular Chemistry will cover. This class explored such areas as behavior and structure of atoms and compounds, arrangement of the periodic table, chemical formulas, types of bonding, chemical reactions, stoichiometry, the study of solids, liquids, and gases, chemical equilibrium, kinetics, thermodynamics, electrochemistry, and an introduction to more specific branches of chemistry such as organic chemistry, biochemistry, and nuclear chemistry. The class included a weekly lab. A traditional lecture format was used in this class, but periodic demonstrations, group work, and discussions were also used. The Council Rock portion of the class was a continuation of the material from Solebury and included the topics and evaluation contained below. The final portion of the class was a one-on-one tutorial with PLC staff member Joel Hammon and consisted of major topics in traditional introductory chemistry that had not been covered so far during the year.

Evaluation: Solebury School provided trimester grades for the portion of the class taken at Solebury. Council Rock homebound instructor provided the following feedback:

Topic	Grade for homework	Grade for test
Chemical equations: writing, balancing, predicting products, classifying, aqueous equations	26/26	43/50
Molar mass, molecular and empirical formulas,	15/16	52/63
Stoichiometry	7/7	44/57
	Summary of grades	187/219 = 85.377%

Biology: (Princeton Learning Cooperative/Self-Study)
Course Description: Study of fundamental concepts, theoretical principles, and practical applications of modern biology with emphasis on biochemistry, genetics, molecular biology, cell biology, and evolution. Biological function at the molecular level was particularly emphasized and covered the structure and regulation of genes, as well as the structure and synthesis of proteins, how these molecules are integrated into cells, and how these cells are integrated into multicellular systems and organisms. The text *Exploring the Way Life Works: The Science of Biology*, by Mahlon Hoagland, Bert Dodson, and Judith Hauck, focuses on the big ideas in biology organized into chapters: Patterns, Energy, Information, Machinery, Feedback, Community, and Evolution. Laboratory exercises stressed the development of skills in basic lab techniques, including observation, measurement, data collection and analysis, and the application and reinforcement of concepts presented in the text: microscope studies, osmosis, diffusion, enzymes, DNA extraction, DNA gel electrophoresis, genetics, macroinvertebrate collection/ID, circulatory

system, and habitat preservation related to threatened or endangered and invasive species. The class took a tour of the Rutgers University cell/DNA Repository.

Text: *Exploring the Way Things Work* by Mahlon Hoagland, Bert Dodson, and Judith Hauck

Material History: (Self-Study)

Course Description: A study of American history through advertising and industry. This course consisted of studying vintage advertising signs, watching shows on material history (American Restoration and American Pickers), engaging in research projects, and participating in hands-on archeological digs. We also visited museums and sales/shows consisting of antique advertising. The research projects consisted of finding information on the history of soda companies and how they came to be, as well as their impact on our society. The finds on the archaeological digs consisted mostly of prohibition era bottles as well as some car parts and pieces of advertising. Trips were taken to Antique Advertising shows and stores including visits to Indianapolis, Ohio, Virginia, Tennessee. Acquaintances of important figures in the field were also acquired, including Irene (and Carter) Davis, author of *Collecting Paint Advertising and Memorabilia*.

Texts Used:

- *Ad Boy* by Warren Dotz and Masud Husain
- *The Fine Art of Collecting and Displaying Petroliana* by Daniel K Matthews
- *Filling Station Collectables* by Rick Pease
- *More Porcelain Enamel Advertising* by Michael Bruner
- *Collecting Paint Advertising and Memorabilia* by Irene Davis
- *Petretti's Coca-Cola Collectables Price Guide*, 12th edition, by Allan Petretti
- *Vernor's Story* by Lawrence Rouch

<u>US History:</u> (Princeton Learning Cooperative/Self-Study)
Course Description: A general survey of United States history from the Civil War through the end of World War II. Particular attention was paid to the history of social movements and various groups inside the United States, how larger global issues impacted US history, and the role technology and geography played in US history. Students were encouraged to use films based on historical themes to extend their study.

Text and Components:

* *A People's History of the United States* by Howard Zinn
* *The American People* by Alan Winkler et al
* Films: *12 Years a Slave, The Butler, A League of Their Own, Great Debaters, Miracle, Tucker,* in addition to others

<u>Geography:</u> (Self-Study)
Course Description: This course is a compilation of various trips taken during high school. The primary experience was a twenty-eight-day European tour. Topics of study during the trip included Jewish culture, Holocaust sites, architecture, local history, and historical and cultural landmarks. Additional trips both inside and outside the United States are also included.

Components:

* Countries visited: Belgium, Netherlands, England, France, Slovenia, Italy, Mexico, Jamaica, US Virgin Islands, Haiti, Bermuda, Dominican Republic, among others.
* States visited: Alaska, Arizona, Michigan, Tennessee, Ohio, Virginia, North Carolina, Indiana, California

<u>Spanish III:</u> (Solebury School/Council Rock/Private Tutor)
Course Description: The first third of the course was taken at Solebury School with the remaining two-thirds completed through Council Rock School

District homebound instruction and a private tutor. Spanish III strengthens and builds on what students have learned in Spanish I and II. After an initial quick review of the first nine units, students worked to finish the textbook *Vistas*, with its accompanying *Supersite*. Students continued to build vocabulary and culture by theme: health, technology, home life, the environment, professions, the arts, and current events. Grammar studies included review and expansion of the tenses they have already learned and an in-depth study of the subjunctive, the use of preterit and imperfect together, relative pronouns, the imperative, present and past perfect tenses, the conditional, and "si" clauses.

Text Used: *Vistas* by Blanco and Donley

Evaluation: Council Rock homebound instructor evaluation: "I have tutored Ethan in Spanish. His grade for the quarter is A. He did very well. Any questions, please contact me."

Small Business: (Self-Study)
Course Description: This course consisted of starting, developing, and maintaining a nonprofit business that raised money for Main Line Animal Rescue. Throughout this course, I developed and practiced skills such as public speaking, marketing, website design, money management, logo design, sales, customer relations, baking (developing recipes), and blanket and toy making. I ran the nonprofit from 2007–present, during which $18,000 was raised for Main Line Animal Rescue. Over the years I have set up shop at around seventy-five craft shows and fairs, with varying results.

Photography: (Solebury School/Self-Study)
Course Description: The majority of this course was taken at Solebury School with continued self-study after leaving Solebury. Photo I was an introductory black-and-white photography class with emphasis on learning the mechanics of a manual exposure camera and the shooting, processing, and printing of

black-and-white negative film. In Photo II the students continued using and refining the shooting, processing, and printing skills learned in Photo I with more emphasis on composition, the effects of aperture and shutter speed, and obtaining good tonal range in the final print.

Introductory Art: (Solebury School/Self-Study)
Course Description: This course is a combination of a ceramics class taken at Solebury and a community-based visual arts class at Art in the Pod studios in Holland, Pennsylvania. Ceramics explored three basic hand-building techniques: pinching (as in pinch pots), coil building, and slab construction. With these three techniques, an artist can create any object that can be imagined. Each skill helps to develop muscle memory and an understanding of the properties of the clay. Timing plays a big part in ceramic work; consequently, students learned how to plan and prepare for every project. The community art class consisted of work in similar techniques, meeting two hours a week for ten weeks.

Cooking: (Princeton Learning Cooperative/Self-Study)
Course Description: This class was based on cooking and baking with seasonal foods while refining knife skills and learning about food safety, recipe reading, and meal planning. The class met for two hours a week. The skills and concepts from the class were then used at home to prepare family meals once a week.

Texts: A variety of cookbooks and Internet-based recipes

Driver's Ed: (Self-Study)
Course Description: I completed an online driver's ed class on the website: http://www.pennsylvaniateendriving.com. The course consisted of over thirty hours of reading and quizzes as well as a final examination. I participated in about twenty lessons with a driving school for 1.5 hours each.

Personal Fitness I: (Self-Study)
Course Description: In this course I actively integrated aspects of personal fitness into daily life, including exercise, nutrition, and mental health, building the daily practices that contribute to staying physically fit. Activities included making healthy food choices, two hours of daily exercise during the fall season as a member of the Solebury School varsity soccer team (two years), and regular exercise as a member of a Futsal team (two years).

Personal Fitness II: (Self-Study)
Course Description: This course was a continuation of Personal Fitness I. Activities included continued work eating a healthy diet, study and exploration of lifestyle choices that best contribute to personal health and fitness, daily exercise (with twice weekly games) as a member of recreational and travel roller hockey leagues (4 years).

3.3. Reading List

This reading list encompasses the books I [Ethan] have read over the last four years and the books I plan to read this year. A few of these books were required for classes, but I read the majority of them voluntarily, according to my interests.

Books I've Read Over the Last Four Years	Author
Lord of the Flies	William Golding
Of Mice and Men	John Steinbeck
A Wrinkle in Time	Madeleine L'Engle
Every Day	David Levithan
To Kill a Mockingbird	Harper Lee
The Life You Can Save	Peter Singer
The Color Purple	Alice Walker
Mountains Beyond Mountains	Tracy Kidder
Othello	William Shakespeare
Hamlet	William Shakespeare
Macbeth	William Shakespeare
1984	George Orwell
The Oedipus Cycle (Oedipus Rex, Oedipus at Colonus, Antigone)	Sophocles (Trans. Dudley Fitts and Robert Fitzgerald)
Siddhartha	Hermann Hesse
Maus I	Art Spiegelman
Maus II	Art Spiegelman
The Wave	Todd Strasser
Things Fall Apart	Chinua Achebe
The Cardturner	Louis Sachar

The Hand of Compassion	Kristen Renwick Monroe

The Great Deluge	Douglas Brinkley
Things Not Seen	Andrew Clements
Speak	Laurie Halse Anderson
Little Brother	Cory Doctorow
Flatland	Edwin Abbott
Perks of Being a Wallflower	Stephen Chbosky
Itch	Simon Mayo
Who Done It?	Jon Scieszka
This Is What Happy Looks Like	Jennifer Smith
The Red Pyramid	Rick Riordan
The Throne of Fire	Rick Riordan
The Serpent's Shadow	Rick Riordan
Vernor's Story	Lawrence Rouch
Chance	Amir D. Aczel
The Future of Us	Jay Asher and Carolyn Mackler
Eggplant Alley	D.M. Cantaneo
The Mysterious Benedict Society	Trenton Lee Stewart
The Mysterious Benedict Society and the Perilous Journey	Trenton Lee Stewart
Knightley & Son	Rohan Gavin

Stupid Fast	Geoff Herbach
I'm With Stupid	Geoff Herbach

Ostrich	Matt Greene
There Is No Dog	Meg Rosoff
Mr. Penumbra's 24-Hour Bookstore	Robin Sloan
Why we Broke Up	Daniel Handler
Inherit the Wind	Jerome Lawrence and Robert Edwin Lee
Persepolis	Marjane Satrapi
Books I Plan to Read this Year	
I Am the Messenger	Markus Zusak
Fahrenheit 451	Ray Bradbury
One+One=Blue	MJ Auch
The Catcher in the Rye	J.D. Salinger
Holes	Louis Sachar
Small Steps	Louis Sachar
Around the World in 100 Days	Gary Blackwood
Itch Rocks	Simon Mayo
Geeks	Jon Katz
The Danger Box	Blue Balliett
The Tragedy Paper	Elizabeth Laban

Eleanor & Park	Rainbow Rowell
The Apothecary	Maile Meloy
Shattering Glass	Gail Giles

Forgive Me, Leonard Peacock	Matthew Quick
Oogy	Larry Levin
Adam Canfield of the Slash	Michael Winerip
Man Made Boy	Jon Skovron
The Mysterious Benedict Society and the Prisoner's Dilemma	Trenton Lee Stewart
The Cheat	Amy Goldman Koss
Bullyville	Francine Prose
Simon Says	Elaine Marie Alphin
Inexcusable	Chris Lynch
Summerland	Michael Chabon
Fooling Houdini	Alex Stone

Acknowledgements

This is the first large writing project I have ever undertaken. I'm shocked by how many people it takes to put together something like this. I'm grateful for the support I've received from everyone listed here and many more that I've forgotten to mention. Kenneth Danford, Catherine Gobron, Susannah Sheffer and everyone else at North Star. Paul Scutt, Alison Snieckus, Katy Burke, Eileen Smyth, Scott Gallagher, MaryBeth Healy and everyone one else involved with Princeton, Bucks and Raritan Learning Cooperatives – teens, families, volunteers, board members and supporters. My cousin Mary Hammon for editing the final draft of the book. Phil Gutis, Justin Lanier and Susannah Sheffer for editing or discussing various portions of earlier incarnations. My teacher friends, students, and family members for reading early drafts and making fantastic suggestions: John Hammon, Marlene Kibler, Anne Harrington, Kai Abis, Joanne Clothier, Justin Freedman, Kate Ambrose, Linda Grayson, Linda Esposti, Mike Burke, Neal Oberto, Sara Lauf, Sue Weber. Matthew Shelley worked on early drafts of the cover design and the website. Matt Chansky for further cover design help. My family – Kerry, Madelyn and Nathan Hammon. Much of this book was written between 4:30 and 6:00am. I'm sure I woke them up many times as I was clomping around downstairs every morning.

About the Author

Joel Hammon is co-founder of The Learning Cooperatives, a group of self-directed learning centers in New Jersey and Pennsylvania. He is also a co-founder of Liberated Learners, an organization dedicated to helping educators create and sustain self-directed learning centers around the world. Joel was a social studies teacher for eleven years in traditional public and private schools. He lives with his family in Langhorne, Pennsylvania and can be reached at me@ joelhammon.com.

CPSIA information can be obtained
at www.ICGtesting.com
Printed in the USA
LVHW022002071221
705523LV00015B/2228